Children's Rights, Educational Research and the UNCRC: past, present and future

Edited by
Jenna Gillett-Swan & Vicki Coppock

SYMPOSIUM
BOOKS

Symposium Books Ltd
PO Box 204, Didcot, Oxford OX11 9ZQ, United Kingdom
www.symposium-books.co.uk

Published in the United Kingdom, 2016

ISBN 978-1-873927-95-3

Printed and bound in the United Kingdom by Hobbs the Printers, Southampton
www.hobbs.uk.com

Children's Rights, Educational Research
and the UNCRC: past, present and future

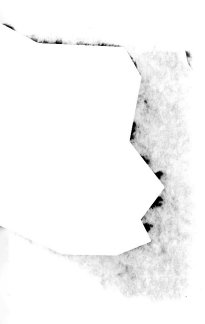

Contents

INTRODUCTION

Children's Rights, Educational Research and the UNCRC

VICKI COPPOCK & JENNA GILLETT-SWAN

SUMMARY On 20 November 1989, the United Nations General Assembly, comprised of delegates representing a wide spectrum of legal systems, cultures and religious traditions, unanimously adopted the Convention on the Rights of the Child (CRC). Now, more than a quarter of a century on, the CRC is ratified by almost the entire international community and is widely regarded as the most important advocacy tool for children's rights. Incorporating the full range of human rights – civil, cultural, economic, political and social – it creates an international legal framework for the protection and promotion of the human rights and fundamental freedoms of all persons under the age of 18. This introductory chapter establishes the motivation and rationale for and aims and objectives of the book and outlines the overarching conceptual framework for the chapters that follow; namely a critical exploration of the ways in which the CRC has informed, presently informs and may in future inform educational research in various contexts internationally. The logic informing the structure of the book is explained and each chapter is introduced, signposting for the reader the key concepts, themes, issues and debates to be covered

On 20 November 1989 the United Nations General Assembly, comprised of delegates representing a wide spectrum of legal systems, cultures and religious traditions, unanimously adopted the Convention on the Rights of the Child (hereafter CRC). Just over a quarter of a century on, the CRC is ratified by almost the entire international community and is widely regarded as the most important advocacy tool for children's rights globally. Incorporating the full range of human rights, civil, cultural, economic, political and social, it creates an international legal framework for the protection and promotion of the human rights and fundamental freedoms of all persons under the age of 18. Even so, while the CRC has provoked significant changes in the way that children's rights are considered, conceptualised and enacted, there is ongoing debate regarding the extent to which the 'children's rights agenda' is embraced fully within societal institutions, as adults, researchers, policy-makers and professionals continue to grapple with actualising the rights enshrined within the CRC in their 'real world' practices (Coppock & Phillips, 2013; Phillips & Coppock, 2014).

Research into children's rights has grown exponentially since the adoption of the CRC in 1989 and is now a legitimate field of study in its own right. Quennerstedt (2014) observes the rapid growth and significance of children's rights research in almost every social science discipline between 1985 and 2012 – research that has 'widened and deepened our knowledge of what rights for children are about' (p. 106). Likewise, Reynaert et al (2009) argue that 'scholarly work on children's rights is almost inconceivable without considering the Convention as the bearer of the children's rights debate' (p. 518). These authors identify three recurrent themes in academic literature on children's rights since the adoption of the CRC and reflect critically on the ways in which these themes have dominated research agendas. The first of these is 'autonomy and participation rights as the new norm in children's rights practice and policy' (Reynaert et al, 2009, p. 520). This arises directly from the requirement of Article 12 of the CRC that States Parties

> assure to the child who is capable of forming his or her own views the right to express those views freely in all matters affecting the child, the views of the child being given due weight in accordance with the age and maturity of the child. (United Nations, 1989, Article 12.1)

Subsequently, a proliferation of research studies has emerged over the past 25 years in which children's views have been sought on various issues affecting their everyday lives. Numerous policy and practice initiatives have been developed that are premised on improving consultation with children, and on the participation of children in the design, delivery and evaluation of services that affect them. Prout (2003) suggests that the mandate to 'listen to children's voices' has become so ubiquitous that it has become part of the 'rhetorical orthodoxy' (p. 11).

Central to this drive towards children's participation rights is recognition of 'the child' as a competent, autonomous 'being' – a conceptual shift usually attributed to the emergence of a new paradigm for the sociology of childhood (James & Prout, 1990; Qvortrup, 1994; Corsaro, 1997). Three key assumptions underpinned this new approach. First, childhood is understood as a *social* rather than a biological construction. In this, the traditional developmental model of childhood is problematised (Burman, 1994). So too is the notion of a 'universal' childhood (Nieuwenhuys, 1998). Second, children are viewed as social actors and, as such, are considered as worthy research *subjects in their own right* and *from their own perspectives* (Alderson, 1993). Third, new epistemological and methodological approaches to research *with* children (Christensen & James, 2000) have informed the 'transition towards recognizing children as "knowers" – able to generate knowledge as well as being the recipients of knowledge, or being the objects of knowledge' (Foley, 2001, pp. 99-100).

A second theme identified by Reynaert et al (2009) in academic literature on children's rights since the adoption of the CRC is the dichotomy between 'children's rights vs. parental rights', and specifically, 'the right of parents to raise their children, on the one hand, and the rights of children to autonomy and self-determination on the other hand' (p. 524). Historically, childhood dependency was codified in law in the form of parental rights, in which the wellbeing of children was assumed to be secure and positive as long as the family fulfilled its obligations. This consensual image was increasingly challenged by those advocating for the recognition and expansion of the legal and moral rights of children and young people in the family (Freeman, 1983; Franklin, 1986). Thus, 'the acknowledgement of the childhood image of the competent child implied that children became visible as a member of the family' (Reynaert et al, 2009, p. 524).

Intervening in the private domain of the family has always been controversial and poses a challenge for the liberal state (Fox Harding, 1996). Traditionally, the state has 'managed' the rights claims of individual family members through its agents – those 'expert' professionals who, under statute, regulate relationships and responsibilities within the family, straddling the split between public and private spheres (Foucault, 1977; Donzelot, 1980; Rose, 1990). However, Reynaert et al (2009) point to the potential detrimental impact of 'rights thinking' in that it focuses attention on individuals rather than on relationships between parents and children, and distracts from wider structural conditions impacting their lives, such as poverty. Moreover, recourse to legal instruments and juridical institutions has created 'antagonistic power relations between children and parents ... [and] functioned as a legitimacy for the state to take over parental responsibilities for the sake of the child' (Vandenbroeck & Bouverne de Bie, cited in Reynaert et al, 2009, p. 526).

The third and final theme identified by Reynaert et al (2009) is that of the dominance of 'the global children's rights industry' (p. 526). The concern here is that 'children's rights have got bogged down in consensus thinking' (p. 527) and that debates around children's rights have been reduced to working out the technicalities of standard setting, implementation and monitoring rather than engaging critically with the *meaning* of children's rights. This 'technicization' of children's rights has negative consequences in that it decontextualises children's rights from children's lived experiences, leading Reynaert et al (2009) to call for a shift towards 'research that provides empirical evidence on the impact that the rhetoric of children's rights has in daily practice' (p. 529).

These three themes, and many of the complex issues, tensions and contradictions arising from them, are (to a greater or lesser extent) evident in the discussions of children's rights, educational research and the UNCRC that make up this volume.

Since its inauguration in 1994 the annual conference of the European Educational Research Association (EERA), the European Conference on Educational Research (ECER), has provided a stimulating and productive environment for researchers committed to the advancement of philosophical, theoretical and empirical knowledge on children's lived experiences of education internationally. EERA's academic work is organised through 32 research networks, with Network 25 specifically dedicated to research on children's rights in education. This network is 'concerned with exploring the ethical, methodological, legal and pedagogical issues that emerge at the intersection of children's rights and educational contexts. A particular focus is the ways in which children's rights provide a provocation to think and practice differently' (ECER Network 25 Descriptor, 2015).[1] Providing an arena for continuous, critical and focused discussion and elaboration on research issues with a bearing on children's rights in educational contexts, the aim is to encourage theoretical and conceptual development in the field of research in children's rights in education.

In recognition of the 25th anniversary of the CRC and inspired by the theme of the ECER 2014 – 'the past, present and future of educational research in Europe' – the editors of this volume led a round-table discussion within Network 25 focused on a critical exploration of the ways in which the UNCRC has informed, presently informs and may in future inform educational research internationally (Coppock & Gillett-Swan, 2014). This edited volume brings together a selection of papers that represent a range of themes, issues and debates that subsequently emerged from those round-table discussions. It is comprised of seven chapters that engage critically with the context, relevance and implications of children's rights, educational research and the CRC internationally, from multiple perspectives. Examples from Australia, Finland, Sweden, Portugal and the United Kingdom represent the diverse and wide-ranging contexts from which the past, present and future of children's rights, educational research and the CRC can be critically examined. Different aspects of children's rights within the context of educational research are scrutinised and problematised and implications for practice considered.

In chapter 1 John I'Anson's explication of some of the critical issues explored by researchers interested in children's rights in education provides a valuable starting point from which the application of the CRC in terms of its varied interpretations and implementation of its core provisions is elaborated. A historical contextualisation of some of the ways in which the CRC has become imbricated with educational research during the past twenty-five years is provided, through which some of the key themes, tropes, orientations and theoretical traditions that have informed children's rights research in education to date are identified. Drawing on Latour (2013), I'Anson observes that while the text of the CRC is the product of a legal mode, it is mobilised in largely extra-legal contexts that cut across the multiple cultures, spaces and discourses that bear upon children's lives. To this extent, I'Anson argues, 'the UNCRC offers a distinctive counterpoint (Brown, 2005) that resists simplification and colonisation whilst insistently raising difficult questions that are at once ethical, political, and existential in scope' (this volume, p. 18). Issues around the theoretical, practical and literal interpretations of children's voice in practice are provided as examples of ways that educational researchers are currently balancing these tensions through their rights-inclusive educational research practices.

The two chapters that then follow take as their focus the subject of children's rights education. In chapter 2 Louise Phillips draws on extensive illustrative material from global contexts to offer a thought-provoking critical analysis of the scope, significance and impact of Article 42 of the CRC, specifically the obligation it imposes on State parties 'to make the principles and provisions of the convention widely known, by appropriate and active means, to adults and children alike' (United Nations, 1989). With schooling compulsory in most countries, it would seem an appropriate and active means to make the CRC widely known to children. Yet, Phillips argues, since the ratification of the CRC in 1989, few nations have endeavoured to include the CRC in mandated curricula. She maps significant actions that have taken place since 1989 to include the CRC within curricula both as an international legal instrument for children and young people to know their rights, and for educators and administrators to support their rights, in policy and practice. Notable gaps, missed opportunities and possible explanations of why embedding the CRC in curricula has been minimal are discussed, along with key actions that hold potential to yield significant influence.

In chapter 3, Nina Thelander presents an analysis and discussion of human rights education with specific reference to how it is practised in Swedish primary schools. She presents findings from an ethnographic research project with primary school teachers in which she explores *what, why and how* the content of human rights education are and could be addressed in schools. Using the threefold definition of human rights education articulated in the World Programme for Human Rights Education (UNCHR, 2005) as a conceptual framework – (i) knowledge and skills; (ii) values, attitudes and behavior and (iii) action – she highlights the centrality of rights education as a key issue supported by discussion of the relevant informing and guiding frameworks that underpin the incorporation of rights education. The global implications and relevance for those seeking to understand rights in practice are demonstrated through acknowledgement of what the future of education that considers human rights at its core may look like. The importance of time and context is highlighted in terms of how these contexts may inform future representations of rights. 'It comprises education *as* a human right and also education *for* human rights' (Thelander, this volume, p. 63), which is something that requires further consideration from multiple stakeholders.

Each of the remaining four chapters explores diverse aspects of the relationship between children's rights, educational research and the CRC. Taking Article 12 of the CRC as their point of departure, Reetta Niemi, Kristiina Kumpulainen and Lasse Lipponen (chapter 4) focus on how the CRC has been enacted in the lived pedagogical practices of Finnish primary school education. Specifically, they ask, 'what does it mean for a child to be heard when it comes to schools and pedagogical practices?' Drawing on empirical data based on an action research initiative collected in one primary classroom community in Helsinki between January 2011 and December 2013, these authors demonstrate how the aspirational goals of the Finnish National Board of Education, in terms of the national core curriculum for pupils' participation in classrooms, are realised in lived pedagogical practices and how these could be expanded into the future. They conclude with a consideration of how learning from the past can guide future educational practices in promoting children's voice and agency in education. Niemi et al's description of the changing face of educational research through engagement, innovation and action research practices invites additional stakeholders to be part of the conversation around children's rights in educational practice. Through showcasing different ways that participation, agency and voice may be enabled in different pedagogical contexts in routine teaching practices, this provides opportunities for a more widespread incorporation and acceptance of children's rights in education.

In chapter 5, Joana Lúcio and Fernando Ilídio Ferreira present an analysis of their research into pre-service teachers' perceptions of their role, and the school's role, as a platform for children's civic and political development. They discuss the issue of children's rights in Portugal in a context of social and economic austerity, across three dimensions – provision, protection and participation – analyzing how children's right to citizenship and civic engagement can become impaired in times of precariousness and social vulnerability. In this, they also discuss the significance of the transformations brought about in initial teacher education by the Bologna Process, which has shown a tendency to saturate teacher training curricula with didactics-related content, to the detriment of the social and cultural aspects of teaching, such as personal and social development and children's participation. They conclude that while the curriculum for initial teacher education in Portugal prepares pre-service teachers adequately in terms of an understanding of the relevance of children's rights, this awareness appears to be purely theoretical in scope, as teachers seem unable to identify explicit instances where children's rights are respected or enforced. Lúcio and Ferreira's findings have significant implications for children's rights in times of economic uncertainty and pressure, providing important lessons for moving forward in terms of progressing a rights agenda, but also in terms of the incorporation and consideration of children's rights in practice for researchers and teachers in education.

Continuing the theme of scrutinising the complexities involved in the work of translation of the CRC into substantive rights for children, Gordon Tait and Mallihai Tambyah (chapter 6) offer a critical analysis of the scope and limitations of the child's right to privacy as articulated in Article 16 of the CRC. They begin with a discussion of the broader conceptual and legal imperatives that frame the issues and debates in this area, moving on to a specific analysis of children's rights to privacy, both in the family and in school. Tait and Tambyah explain that the notion of 'privacy' is a complex one and, far from being an essential human right and requirement, appears to be historical and culturally contingent. Through their discussion of 'childhood as a regulated space', they demonstrate how the 'right to privacy' and the 'needs of government' (that is, routine state-sanctioned practices of supervision and surveillance of children in the home and at school) often work in opposition to one another. This leads them to question whether Article 16 is of any value to children, and whether, at best, the CRC is a symbolic benchmark for framing debates pertaining to childhood.

In focusing on the past, present and future of children's rights in educational research we share Bobbio's (1996) view that 'the Convention must be seen as a historical and political document, not as children's rights set in stone' (Quennerstedt, 2014, p. 111). That is, 'ideas about children's rights [must] be linked with constructions of children and childhood, embedded in time- and place-bound discourses, rather than a once-and-for-all essential view on rights' (Hagglund & Thelander, 2011, p. 368). Veerman's (2014) analysis of the ageing of the CRC illustrates the point forcefully and convincingly. There are many aspects of contemporary experiences of children and childhood that were quite literally inconceivable to the drafters of the Convention – perhaps most notably the scope, scale and influence of the global expansion of digital technologies. Thus, in the final chapter of this volume we, the editors, consider the impact and significance of the exponential growth of digital technologies for children's rights and educational research. We observe how children's engagement with digital media is an underdeveloped, but increasingly important field for those researching children's rights in educational contexts. Using the conceptual framework of the CRC's '3 Ps', we identify and critically explore emerging themes, issues and debates relating to children's rights in education arising from children's engagement with digital and social media. Taking a future-oriented perspective, we conclude with some critical reflections on how digital technologies may reform children's rights research internationally, highlighting prospects and possibilities in developing future educational research agendas and practices.

Times have changed and are still changing, and this, Veerman (2014) argues, 'makes the Convention look "old"' (p. 42). The ageing of the United Nations Convention on the Rights of the Child poses significant challenges for researchers of children's rights generally, and for researchers of children's rights in education specifically, in that research agendas must push the boundaries of what is deemed 'relevant'. The need for researchers to respond to the ever-changing world of children's rights through continuous examination and re-examination of the opportunities and tensions within the CRC is a central theme in this edited collection. What becomes increasingly clear is that it is no longer justifiable (if indeed it ever was) for researchers of children's rights to stay rooted in the CRC of 1989. Rather, we must look toward future developments and considerations of children's rights in educational research and practice. Crucially, we must 'stretch beyond an understanding of the Convention as a document where "curriculum-like" norms for what constitutes children's rights are formulated' (Hagglund & Thelander, 2011, p. 368). This is vital if research on children's rights in education is to make a significant contribution to the reimagining children's human rights in the twenty-first century and beyond.

Note

[1] http://www.eera-ecer.de/networks/network25/

References

Alderson, P. (1993) *Children's Consent to Surgery.* Buckingham: Open University Press.

Bobbio, N. (1996) *The Age of Rights.* Cambridge: Polity Press.

Brown, W. (2005) *Edgework: critical essays on knowledge and politics.* Princeton, NJ: Princeton University Press.

Burman, E. (1994) *Deconstructing Developmental Psychology.* London: Routledge.

Christensen, P. & James, A. (Eds) (2000) *Research with Children: perspectives and practices.* London: Falmer Press.

Coppock, V. & Gillett-Swan, J. (2014) *The UNCRC at 25. Critical Reflections on its Influence and Impact on Educational Research; Past, Present and Future.* Round Table, European Conference on Educational Research (ECER), *The Past, Present and Future of Educational Research in Europe*, University of Porto, Portugal, 5 September.

Coppock, V. & Phillips, L. (2013) Editorial. Actualization of Children's Participation Rights Part 1, *Global Studies of Childhood*, Special Issue: Actualization of Children's Participation Rights Part 1, 3(2), 99-103 (http://dx.doi.org/10.2304/gsch.2013.3.2.99).

Corsaro, W. (1997) *The Sociology of Childhood*. Thousand Oaks, CA: Pine Forge Press.

Donzelot, J. (1980) *The Policing of Families*. London: Hutchinson.

Foley, P. (2001) 'Our Bodies, Ourselves'?: mothers, children and health care at home, in P. Foley, J. Roche & S. Tucker (Eds) *Children in Society*. Basingstoke: Palgrave.

Foucault, M. (1977) *Discipline and Punish: the birth of the prison*. London: Allen & Unwin.

Fox Harding, L. (1996) *Family, State and Social Policy*. London: Macmillan. http://dx.doi.org/10.1007/978-1-349-24377-8

Franklin, B. (Ed.) (1986) *The Rights of Children*. London: Blackwell.

Freeman, M.D.A. (1983) *The Rights and Wrongs of Children*. London: Frances Pinter.

Hagglund, S. & Thelander, N. (2011) Children's Rights at 21: policy, theory, practice. Introductory Remarks, *Education Inquiry*, 2(3), 365-372. http://dx.doi.org/10.3402/edui.v2i3.21988

James, A. & Prout, A. (1990) *Constructing and Reconstructing Childhood*. London: Falmer Press.

Latour, B. (2013) *An Inquiry into Modes of Existence: an anthropology of the moderns*. Cambridge, MA: Harvard University Press.

Nieuwenhuys, O. (1998) Global Childhood and the Politics of Contempt, *Alternatives: Global, Local, Political*, 23, 267-290.

Phillips, L. & Coppock, V. (2014) Editorial. Actualisation of Children's Participation Rights Part 2, *Global Studies of Childhood*, Special Issue: Actualisation of Children's Participation Rights Part 2, 4(2), 59-63. http://dx.doi.org/10.2304/gsch.2014.4.2.59

Prout, A. (2003) Participation, Policy and the Changing Conditions of Childhood, in C. Hallett & A. Prout (Eds) *Hearing the Voices of Children: social policy for a new century*. London: RoutledgeFalmer. http://dx.doi.org/10.4324/9780203464618_chapter_1

Quennerstedt, A. (2014) Children's Rights Research Moving into the Future – Challenges on the Way Forward, in M. Freeman (Ed.) *The Future of Children's Rights*. Leiden: Brill Nijhoff. http://dx.doi.org/10.1163/9789004271777_007

Qvortrup, J. (1994) Childhood Matters: an introduction, in J. Qvortrup, M. Bardy, G. Sgritta & H. Wintersberger (Eds) *Childhood Matters: social theory, practice and politics.* Aldershot: Avebury Press.

Reynaert, D., Bouverne-de Bie, M. & Vandevelde, S. (Eds) (2009) A Review of Children's Rights Literature since the Adoption of the United Nations Convention on the Rights of the Child, *Childhood*, 16(4), 518-534. http://dx.doi.org/10.1177/0907568209344270

Rose, N. (1990) *Governing the Soul: the shaping of the private self.* London: Routledge.

United Nations (1989) *The United Nations Convention on the Rights of the Child (UNCRC).* General Assembly resolution 44/25, 20 Nov. 1989. UN Doc. A/RES/44/25. http://www.ohchr.org/en/professionalinterest/pages/crc.aspx

United Nations Commission on Human Rights (UNCHR) (2005) World Programme for Human Rights Education (2005–ongoing). http://www.ohchr.org/EN/Issues/Education/Training/Pages/Programme.aspx (accessed 21 December 2015).

Veerman, P.E. (2014) The Ageing of the UN Convention on the Rights of the Child, in M. Freeman (Ed.) *The Future of Children's Rights.* Leiden: Brill Nijhoff.

CHAPTER 1

UNCRC at 25: a critical assessment of achievements and trajectories with reference to educational research

JOHN I'ANSON

SUMMARY This chapter offers a historical contextualisation of some of the ways in which the UNCRC has become imbricated with educational research during the past 25 years. It identifies some of the key themes, tropes, orientations and theoretical traditions that have informed children's rights research to date, with particular reference to education. While the text of the UNCRC is the product of a legal mode, it is mobilised in largely extra-legal contexts that cut across the multiple cultures, spaces and discourses that bear upon children's lives. To this extent, the UNCRC offers a distinctive counterpoint that resists simplification and colonisation whilst insistently raising difficult questions that are at once ethical, political and existential in scope. Some of the ways in which such issues have been taken up in the context of educational research are considered along with a consideration of some of the tensions to which this gives rise. The trope of counterpoint is then taken up as a means of exploring possible future trajectories that work beyond some of the limitations associated with practices of critique.

Introduction

This chapter considers of some of the ways in which the United Nations Convention on the Rights of the Child (UNCRC) (United Nations, 1989) has become imbricated with educational research during the past twenty-five years. More specifically, the intention is to explore critically how the UNCRC has informed, presently informs and may in future inform educational research internationally. This involves identifying some of the key themes, tropes, orientations and theoretical traditions that have together informed children's rights research to date, with particular reference to education. Having identified some of the tensions that inform these trajectories to date, it should then be possible to suggest some productive directions of travel.

Since its formal inauguration in 1989, the UNCRC has become the most ratified of all conventions (Tisdall & Punch, 2012, p. 250). Although it was the outcome of ten years of deliberation before formal agreement was reached, the formation of the convention can be traced back to the Second World War (Hägglund & Thelander, 2011; Mayall, 2012). While the text of the UNCRC is the product of a legal mode (Latour, 2013), it is mobilised in largely extra-legal contexts that cut across the multiple cultures, spaces and discourses that bear upon children's lives. To this extent, the UNCRC offers a distinctive counterpoint (Brown, 2005) that may resist simplification and colonisation, while insistently raising difficult questions that are at once ethical, political and existential in scope. Some of the ways in which such issues have been taken up in the context of educational research will be considered along with an exploration of some of the problematics to which this gives rise. The trope of counterpoint is then proposed as a means of exploring possible future trajectories that work beyond some of the limitations associated with practices of critique.

Given the potential scope of such a review, this has been limited to a consideration of issues and themes identified and taken up in papers given within the Research in Children's Rights in Education network [1] at the European Conference on Educational Research (ECER), so as to identify a number of issues and concerns that have exercised researchers in this field (see ECER, 2015).

The UNCRC and the Work of Translation

The analysis begins by identifying the UNCRC as a specific kind of text: it is the product of a legal mode (Evans, 2005; Latour, 2013). A legal mode has certain affordances, in terms of its universal appeal and especially in terms of its authority to insist upon certain obligations. Thus, for example, states that are signatories to the convention are required to report every five years on how they have complied with rights and obligations under that requirement (see UK Government, 2008). However, since its inception in 1989 it has also been necessary for the UNCRC to be translated into other-than-legal modes of existence that might become mobilised in ways that cut across multiple cultures, spaces and discourses that bear upon children's lives.

As we will see below, some of the tensions, elisions and problematics that arise in the field of children's rights do so because this work of translation is either ignored or regarded as unproblematic: *how* the articles are translated into specific professional practices, institutions and forms of accountability, and so forth, is a key question. Once a translation has been achieved it often becomes invisible; a case in point is the ease with which we click on a mouse to gain information about a particular topic or issue on our computers. But as Latour (2013) has observed, this 'double-click' of the mouse hides all the decisions along the way, hidden from view, that have been made as to which information is relevant and which particular translation is to be preferred. This even includes semantic and performative issues that derive from data coding which – while also invisible in the act of searching – nevertheless exercise influence and constraint in terms of the meaning and ordering of what is presented (Edwards & Carmichael, 2012). A forgetfulness of the complexity of mediations and translations certainly makes life simpler, but it also leads to difficulties from a more critical perspective, especially when utterances from one mode, such as a legal mode, are translated into those of another, whether this be politics or morality, for example. So how good are these translations and what kinds of research has this provoked?

This work of translation has taken multiple forms, and has led to a series of productive engagements with other fields. For example, the UNCRC necessarily intersects with political theory, in so far as children's rights involve the 'problematic of negotiating the powers and values of enduring collectivities' (Brown, 2005, p. 75). Rights talk has implications for governmentality, and there have been critical readings of policy in the light of this, most recently in relation to government anti-radicalisation policy, for example (Coppock, 2002; Coppock & McGovern, 2014). Given the focus on empirical situations of practice, there has been a strong ethnographic focus, especially as regards the use of case studies (Mannion & I'Anson, 2004), such as children's use of digital technologies (e.g. I'Anson, 2011). Meanwhile, a broader range of educational theory has, in recent years, been brought to bear, regarding research within formal schooling contexts, within after school facilities, and within children's broader geographies. Linked to this has been a concern with ethical and moral implications of work with the UNCRC.

1. Orienting Tropes

(i) Voice

Educational research in children's rights to date has drawn upon a number of distinct tropes. Perhaps the most well-known example is that of 'voice', no doubt prompted in large part by the explicit incorporation of the child's right to express views and have these taken seriously in Article 12 of the UNCRC. Notwithstanding the continuing presence of 'voice' as a trope within children's rights discourse, some of the dilemmas this gives rise to have been a focus at both professional and theoretical levels (e.g. in law and ethnography, Griffiths & Kandel, 2000; in education and ethnography, James, 2007; I'Anson, 2013). In some research, the representation of 'the child's voice' appears as an unproblematic achievement; however, more critical investigations have inquired into how the voice that is presented in a given text has been produced: to what extent have children, for example, been involved in the final redaction of the text, where it is easy for the (decontextualised) presentation of themes and illustrations to support a particular writer's narrative, rather than this necessarily being what the children and young people might themselves have intended.

Furthermore, the notion of 'voice' might itself be somewhat problematic, given that it appears to assume – and produce – precisely the kind of autonomous western individualism that has become subject to critique in so much recent writing. The complicity of rights discourse with conditions and disciplinary logics associated with market economies has also been the subject of trenchant critique (Evans, 2005). There may well be strategic reasons for promoting such autonomy as a means of presenting the child as a competent actor, but this not only runs into theoretical difficulties, it can also create binary oppositions, such as competition with other rights bearers, such as parents and educators (Morrow, 1999; Reynaert et al, 2009). So a trope that at first appears to be relatively unproblematic, and a means of marking a changed image of childhood, begins to unravel and to raise far-reaching questions, once this becomes subject to critical review.

(ii) Participation

The trope of 'participation' has also gained currency within research literature in recent years (Mannion et al, 2015) and this has enabled links with sister fields of study such as inclusion, social justice, and work on children's civic participation (Francia, 2013; Lúcio & I'Anson, 2015). The foregrounding of participation (which is also aligned with Article 12 of the UNCRC) reflects a relational focus that has been a significant concern within research.

Mobilisation of children's rights is usually oriented to a text – that of the UNCRC – and this can lead to a privileging of dynamics associated with a 'grammar of representation' (Candler, 2006). This can be characterised as a relational economy in which an independent text is foregrounded that becomes the arbiter and measure of truth. In other words, the focus is upon the ways in which a particular text is mobilised and descriptions are orientated to that. This can be contrasted with a 'grammar of participation' (Candler, 2006). Here, relations within a particular site are foregrounded; knowledge and insight emerge fundamentally in and through the ongoing exploration of those relations. It is towards such a grammar that studies focused upon participation tend to gravitate, rather than one based upon a grammar of representation. Studies oriented to participation also, *inter alia*, tend to focus upon the qualities of relations that enable children and young people to thrive – in some cases in ways beyond what might otherwise have been expected from the demographic data available. The trope of participation also orients attention to the different spaces of children's participation, with a recognition that children's geographies are complex and cannot be assumed in advance of empirical investigation (e.g. Holt, 2011).

(iii) Ecological Perspectives

More recently still, an interest has emerged in linking children's rights research with the trope of 'ecology', which has served to foreground analyses informed by place, values informing sustainability, and relational ontologies. An ecological perspective informs Mannion and Gilbert's (2015, p. 228) account of intergenerational relations which is predicated upon two interconnected premises: (1) people and places are reciprocally enmeshed and co-emergent, and (2) people learn through making embodied responses to differences.

A broad range of educational theorists, geographers and anthropologists, among others, have taken up broadly socio-material traditions of theorising (Fenwick et al, 2011; Sorensen, 2011; Fenwick & Landri, 2014) that seek to acknowledge process and co-emergence in a variety of different ways. Thus Ingold's work (2003, 2011), for example, which has been drawn upon in a number of papers given within ECER Network 25, explores some of the implications in working beyond binaries such as culture and nature, and instead situates relations within a unified field that focuses upon how people and place are relationally co-emergent.

A concern with, and the acknowledgement of, inter-generational relations in relation to rights-informed practice has also emerged in recent years, especially in relation to policy, given the increased involvement of children and young people with this (Mannion, 2012). Thus in their research, Mannion and Gilbert (2015, p. 229) noted 'the importance of reciprocity of relations between generations, and the importance of "place" in everyday embodied encounters between different generational members'. Within these terms, intergenerational learning is constituted in and through relational differences between generations and between people and the places they inhabit.

Research in intergenerational relations includes discussion of some of the professional dilemmas that have surfaced within specific contexts, such as within physical education (PE). Here, according to research carried out by Öman and Quennerstedt (2015), avoidance of intergenerational touch is increasingly being justified through reference to the children's rights agenda and the protection of children from harm. In their paper, Öman and Quennerstedt (2015, p. 1) develop an alternative approach 'from the vantage point of children's human right to develop to their full potential, which can support a need for physical touch in pedagogical situations'. The paper both foregrounds some of the dilemmas that accrue from taking an inter-generational perspective and also addresses the issue of situations in practice where different rights, taken in isolation, can lead to conflicting outcomes.

Intergenerational relations also have significant consequences for thinking about citizenship especially as regards implications for multigenerational citizenship and its relevance for children (e.g. Van Bueren, 2011).

2. Some Directions of Travel

It is possible to identify a number of key directions of travel within educational research and children's rights in recent years.

(i) International Comparison

International comparison between specific national contexts and regions has led to work on standard setting (Reynaert et al, 2009), policy and practice (Thelander, 2009; Quennerstedt, 2011; Harcourt & Hägglund, 2013) together with accounts of progress in implementation as between different contexts. Differences in regional emphasis have also been a focus for consideration. Thus Quennerstedt (2011), for example, compared the implementation of rights in Sweden and New Zealand, taking into account the difference in social, cultural and historical conditions, and found a number of similarities, such as the extension of children's rights to include pre-school (even though this is not a formal requirement of the convention). Another similarity described by Quennerstedt (2011) was that both nations employ a rights-based approach to the learning of knowledge and skills and the forming of values. The respective policies acknowledged that equal access to education for all is not sufficient in itself to meet the right to education per se. Beyond this, however, a number of differences derive from the socio-political context where the emphasis in New Zealand is upon equality in terms of bi-culturality, whereas in Sweden the focus is upon induction into explicitly social democratic values and practices. These contrasting cultural contexts therefore inflect differently how rights are interpreted and mobilised in each respective context.

Also of note within a broader consideration of children's rights research in an international context is a critical reading of the discourse in so far as this contributes to a marked imbalance between Majority and Minority childhoods. Here, the dangers that a single, universal category of 'childhood' can bring in its trail have been identified, especially from researchers working within development studies. In particular, within a western context, it is too easy to assume that children's experience – where case studies instantiate children exercising particular kinds of autonomy and agency – are representative of Majority world contexts. According to Tisdall and Punch (2012, p. 259), 'Minority World conceptualisations of childhood, and children's rights in particular, suggest an individual that [is] detached from the reciprocity, responsibilities and relationships embedded in various cultural contexts.'

Such a critique has far-reaching implications for research and suggests that it is necessary to 'bracket' a number of assumptions that are usually associated with a rights perspective so as to acknowledge indigenous constructions that may foreground different values and relations. To this extent, a simple focus upon children and young people's perspectives, agency and participation is no longer sufficient and a more fine-grained approach that registers 'the intricacies, complexities, tensions, ambiguities and ambivalences of children and young people's lives' (Tisdall & Punch, 2012, p. 259) in both Majority and Minority World contexts is necessary.

(ii) Extending Rights

A further theme has been that of extending the reach of rights, especially as regards children's engagement in the research process. One area is children's rights and early years practice, where, according to Harcourt (2011, p. 335), such work is predicated upon the assumption of competence in line with principles from the UNCRC: 'Designing the research process to include children as active research participants and collaborators recognises the inherent competence that children can offer.' In her research work with children aged between three and five, Harcourt (2011, p. 338), through the use of innovative research practice (such as using an adaptation of a 'mosaic approach' [Clark, 2001] that draws upon multiple forms of data, including drawings, texts, conversations and photographs), found that children demonstrated research expertise and were, moreover, 'articulate authorities on life as a child'. This in turn led to a significant disjunction between children's *apparent* experience – as constructed by adults – and that which they themselves described using such approaches. Furthermore, the state of adulthood was itself understood differently from the children's perspective: a re-positioning that has yet to be acknowledged in research framings (Harcourt, 2011, p. 338). Such work with early years children presents some new ethical issues and challenges that have also become a focus of renewed attention (e.g. Sargeant & Harcourt, 2012).

A further way in which the discourse of rights has been extended is through the acknowledgement and engagement with what might be termed 'neglected articles'. Much of the work to date in the field has focused upon UNCRC Articles 4 and 12 in particular, but more recently there is evidence of a new concern with engaging articles that have not so far been at the forefront – such as Articles 28 and 29, which are explicitly concerned with education and values.

(iii) Proliferation of Theory

While research in relation to the UNCRC remains strongly influenced by theories associated with the New Sociology of Childhood (Jenks, 1982; Qvortrup et al, 1994; James & Prout, 1997; James et al, 1998), in recent years there is evidence of some researchers drawing upon a broader range of theoretical commitments. This derives in part from a problematisation of theoretical assumptions informing the 'new' sociology of childhood/childhood studies approach which emerged over twenty years ago (e.g. Tisdall & Punch, 2012), but also from a recognition of the affordances of other traditions of inquiry.

The New Sociology of Childhood emerged at much the same time as the UNCRC and was immediately to hand as a theoretical framing that legitimised a concern with children's agency and expression, especially as regards children's present lives as worthy of concern. This approach to theorising has become – and remains – highly influential especially in studies conducted in Scandinavia, the UK, central and southern Europe, and Australia, etc. In recent years, papers within ECER Network 25 have begun to draw upon a wider range of other traditions of theorising in the literature, such as capabilities theory (Nussbaum & Sen, 1999), relational ethics (Gilligan, 1982; Arneil, 2002), together with an acknowledgement of other European educational traditions, such as *Bildung* and *Didactics* (Biesta, 2011, 2014) and indeed – although much less frequently – other-than-European traditions. A number of papers have drawn upon Freire and, more often still, Foucault, so as to exercise a critical reading of sites and texts, whether this be an analysis of relational dynamics in a classroom, or an investigation of gendered images within school textbooks.

However, a number of commentators have argued that much research work in children's rights has been theoretically unadventurous and somewhat limited to date, and have remarked on the desirability of new theoretical questions and explorations (Reynaert et al, 2012; Quennerstedt, 2013).

3. Tensions within the Field

In this section three tensions within the field are identified in relation to advocacy versus criticality, the forms of accountability produced, and different ontological assumptions that are implied in research work.

(i) Advocacy and Criticality

During this period a number of tensions have merged within the field. One such tension is that between the roles of advocacy for rights-informed approaches versus the role of critique in relation to the concepts, theories and assumptions that are mobilised in practice. Such a dividing line is clearly apparent in relation to discussions regarding the 'voice' of children and young people, already mentioned in relation to dominant tropes (see 1.i. above). On the one hand, there is a compelling need to hear the voice of children in relation to a wide range of issues that are of concern to them. On the other hand, this activist agenda may sit uneasily alongside those whose role it is to take a critical vantage point vis-à-vis questions as to whose voice is being presented and how this is produced (James, 2007). Much of the research, as noted in the section on the proliferation of research (2.iii., above), remains linked to a distinct 'western' rights agenda that foregrounds autonomy and agency over, for example, a concern with negotiated interdependencies (Tisdall & Punch, 2012). Furthermore, a critical perspective might also point to a tendency in some accounts to silence material dimensions that co-produce voice, alongside adult redaction practices that refract a child's voice in particular ways, as we have seen.

A further way in which this tension between advocacy and critique is manifested derives from the very success with which children's rights has become established and institutionalised within a wide range of organisations during the past 25 years.

While the 'success' of the UNCRC approach globally might be measured through its imbrication within an increasing number of organisations and contexts, critics have raised a number of concerns that include questioning the process of institutionalisation that extends the reach of rights, and these concerns also problematise the production of the UNCRC text itself.

In relation to the institutionalisation of rights, some commentators have voiced concern with ways in which the promulgation of rights-informed approaches is linked to educationalisation (*Pädagogisierung*) through which children have become increasingly subject to adults' pedagogical oversight and control via the increased professionalisation of education (Depaepe, 1998; Reynaert et al, 2009). According to this line of critique, children's everyday practices have become increasingly subsumed within adult pedagogy. One of the implications of the 'new' or extended professionalism – such as that advocated by Sachs (2003), for example, that argues for the role of a teacher extending beyond a limited concern with the curriculum (and which is usually presented as an unquestioned good) – is the possibility that it may in turn issue in *unintended* consequences through its contribution to greater oversight of children by adults. In practice, the extension of adult educational responsibility can lead to a series of professional dilemmas too (Allan et al, 2005).

From an anthropological perspective, concerns have been voiced that such 'educationalisation' in respect of rights is a further extension of nineteenth-century quests to 'civilise the south' through programmes of colonisation (Valentin & Meinert, 2009). Here, the authors are seeking to disturb some of the assumptions regarding normativity and the universal ambitions implied by the rights agenda especially in regard to notions of 'proper' childhood and adulthood. To this extent, according to Valentin and Meinert (2009, p. 23), 'the civilizing project is obviously not confined to today's children only, but reflects a historical process in which children have – perhaps increasingly – become objects for adult and institutional intervention'.

As regards the problematisation of the UNCRC, there is some irony that a text that calls for children's broader participation and expression was itself produced through a process in which children were conspicuous by their absence. To that extent, it is clearly not the outcome of an intergenerational process and this leads to questions as to how different a text that *did* attend to the voices of children (in both Majority and Minority worlds) might be, and what form this might take. Related to this are further questions concerning how a successor discourse to the present UNCRC text might conceivably be produced.

(ii) Accountability Agendas

Linked to these concerns is a tension that arises from a perceived need to mobilise rights versus concerns about how such a translation takes place in practice, and what its consequences are in terms of accountability. As Robinson (2014b, p. 18, emphasis added) observes, embedding 'articles into educational policy documents is no guarantee that they will be translated into practices grounded in demonstrating respect for pupils; *it is the manner in which these rights are interpreted and upheld* that is of significance'.

This work of translation has proceeded at an astonishing pace since the formal launching of the UNCRC in 1989. Indeed, in this connection, Stammers (1999, p. 991) refers to 'the global children's rights industry' in so far as there has been an enormous amount of time and energy spent on constructing instruments for 'standard setting, monitoring and reporting, enforcement, and interventions' such that rights becomes instituted as international public law. In view of its universalising scope, Reynaert et al (2009, pp. 526ff.) in their review of literature take up this 'global children's rights industry' as one of the three key themes that they identify.

Here too, the imbrication of rights-based practice within audit cultures (Power, 1999; Strathern, 2000; Ranson, 2003) raises far-reaching political questions concerning the *kinds* of translations that take place, especially when this appears to be resolved into a series of performative statements, or 'indicators'. In this connection, Thede (2001) has raised significant concerns as to how, precisely, these translations between rights and indicators are effected, pointing to the tendency for the process of fabrication to become invisible once it has been made. In Thede's (2001, p. 259) words:

> The contested nature of any particular measurement is such
> that the consolidation of several measurements into an 'index'
> for comparative purposes is risky and misleading. Our
> approach to quantitative measurement is therefore highly
> circumspect. In addition to ... [a number of] practical problems
> ... there is a disquieting lack of theory concerning the
> translation of a 'right' into a measurement.

These instruments for measurement are the performative means through which adult accountability agendas in relation to children's rights are produced. The various performance indicators that are constructed as a consequence become the specific textual forms through which the rights agenda is mobilised and adult responsibilities discharged. While this enables organisations to measure the extent to which particular agendas have been achieved, there are critical questions to be asked concerning the kinds of translations that are being performed and the ethical limitations inherent in such economies of practice.

(iii) Different Research Ontologies

At a theoretical level, some of the tensions that are played out within research in children's rights are informed by different ontologies. For example, the decision as to whether to focus upon a particular entity such as 'the child' or upon the relations that co-produce 'the child' is likely to have far-reaching consequences as regards the kind of analysis and conclusions that are reached. Here, a focus upon the 'child' and 'young people' will tend towards a substance ontology, which, in terms of analysis, begins with distinct entities. A concern with 'voice' in this context fits well within this way of making sense. So, for example, a focus on tensions between children and parents, even if the social construction of childhood is acknowledged, can still be treated in ways that privilege particular entities. However, approaches such as those informing ecological perspectives (1.iii above) draw upon relational ontologies instead. Here, the focus is not upon a particular entity, but upon the relations that constitute a particular event or assemblage. Both the theoretical resources drawn upon and the directions of travel in terms of analysis as between a substance and a relational ontology differ quite markedly.

A further ontological difference that can be marked concerns the understandings of the child and childhood that are drawn upon in different mobilisations of rights. Where the limits and possibilities of childhood are *assumed to be known already*, this implies an ontological identification of the real with what is actual; what can come to pass is *limited by* that which is already present. As Deleuze (1988, p. 98, italics in the original) put this, 'we give ourselves a real that is ready-made, preformed, pre-existent to itself, and that will pass into existence according to an order of successive limitations. Everything is already *completely given.*' With such an account, the process of evolution, for example, is regarded as consisting simply in the unfolding of *what is already given*, and this involves a progression towards some pre-established end. Nothing new enters the scene: the limits of what is possible are given in advance.

In direct contrast, a virtual ontology is one in which there is always a possibility of surprise: the future is open to a new play of differences and becomings that are not constrained by what has already come to pass (the actual) – which is always only one particular instantiation of a set of possibilities (the virtual). For Deleuze (1988), the virtual is to be distinguished from mere possibility, since possibility is usually imagined on the basis of what is known or assumed to be the case already. As Colebrook (2002, p. 97) observed, 'possibility is a pale and imagined version of the actual world, [whereas] virtual difference and becoming is the very power of the world'. Virtual potentiality can be regarded as a field from which any given actual becomes realised. As such, any given (actual) real can be regarded as a limitation of the virtual. In so far as *this* ontological orientation is mobilised, therefore, children's becomings remain undecidable: it is not known in advance what will come to pass, where a new and unforeseen assemblage of relations, for example, creates a new state of affairs. There is, in principle, an open field of becoming. Such an ontology may inform empirical investigations to the extent that they do not foreclose what may happen in advance, but the rhetoric of certainty that informs most research councils means that, at least in so far as a researcher's initial application is concerned, they will tend to be committed to framings that identify the real with the actual, rather than to more experimental and open-ended empirical orientations.

4. Looking to the Future

In this section a number of future orientations are identified in relation to the trope of counterpoint, the anthropology of the good and impact agendas; these draw upon, and take further, points raised in previous sections.

(i) Counterpoint

While a critical perspective might be seen as an advance over what is perceived by academics to be an uncritical appropriation and mobilisation of rights discourse, Latour (2004) has voiced some misgivings over how critique is performed – and its consequences. Thus, in his influential paper 'Has Critique Run Out of Steam?' Latour (2004) points to ways in which critique often projects assumptions onto another and is consequently unable to move beyond this point of departure. A self-fulfilling cycle is created that leads to a theory becoming invulnerable. Traditional approaches to critique involve one 'side' as necessarily being positioned as counter to or potentially subsumed by its other. As such, the practice of critique is viewed in oppositional terms, with participants involved in some kind of agonistic struggle. There is, in this scenario, a failure of generosity with respect to an alternative perspective's affordances, coupled with a denial of the limitations that necessarily accompany any given standpoint.

Perhaps one way forward is through engaging an alternative, more eirenic metaphor – that of counterpoint, as developed by the political theorist Wendy Brown (2005). Here, the aim is not to provide an exhaustive, 'knock-down' analysis, but to identify particular themes that have been productive, while acknowledging the limits of a particular approach. Such a concern with identifying limitations in the theories that are taken up – together with the knowledges that are thereby produced – mirrors empirical scientific practice and has resonances with traditions of thinking such as the *via negativa* in contemplative practice (Knorr Cetina, 1999). Such acts of diplomacy are a condition of possibility for dialogical imaginaries, where mutual exchange that values difference and heterogeneity is valorised.[2] In this connection, according to Brown (2005, p. 74), counterpoint 'complicates a single or dominant theme through the addition of contrasting themes or forces'. She continues:

> At once open-ended and tactical, counterpoint emanates from
> and promotes an anti hegemonic sensibility and requires a
> modest and carefully styled embrace of multiplicity in which
> contrasting elements, featured simultaneously, do not simply
> war, harmonize, blend, or compete but rather bring out

complexity that cannot emerge through a monolithic or single melody.

Such a 'carefully styled embrace of multiplicity' may well offer productive ways of engaging the multiple stakeholders within the field of children's rights in the years to come. This would involve valorising the heterogeneity, difference and multiplicity of perspectives that have characterised the field of children's rights research for the past 25 years. Engaging with the implications of such a metaphor might go some way towards realising a 'politics of imaginative generosity' as described by Thrift (2004).

How might a metaphor of counterpoint touch down in practice? The UNICEF UK 'Rights Respecting Schools Award' (RRSA) is one initiative that through a specific programme aims to foster 'good' practice and then to confer an award once this has been attained. Formal evaluations of such initiatives have been positive, with pupils reporting a number of improvements in relations, in their feeling of belonging, and to overall school ethos (Robinson, 2013, 2014a). According to Sebba and Robinson's (2010) research, embedding a rights-respecting language within a school enables pupils and staff to work towards mutually respectful and tolerant outcomes even when dealing with issues where there is potential disagreement.

However, Sebba and Robinson (2010, p. 40) also identify a number of limitations with this approach, for although the young people interviewed thought certain issues were important, they tended to be somewhat peripheral to what were taken as being central to school policy priorities. Robinson (2014b, p. 19) has subsequently raised a number of ethical concerns regarding the kinds of decisions over which children and young people are permitted to deliberate:

> While on the surface relationships may appear to be mutually
> respectful, the micro-processes at play within schools can
> work to position pupils as relatively 'powerless' when
> compared to the adults in schools, with pupils internalising
> unstated assumptions that certain aspects of school
> organisation, policies and practices are not open to be
> challenged by them.

A second concern related to the extent to which all young peoples' views were entertained and respected equally. The issue here, according to Robinson (2014b, p. 19), is whether young people who hold values that are aligned with what adults want to hear are more likely to be listened to (and listened to respectfully) as compared with young people whose views run counter to what a school promotes, and who lack the kinds of cultural capital that is valued. The danger here is that individuals in the latter category are more likely to be marginalised and have their views overlooked as compared with those who espouse views congruent with those held by the adults in the school.

Having acknowledged that, in practice, the hoped-for mutuality of respectful adult–pupil relations may not be quite as present or inclusive as at first envisaged, Robinson (2014b, p. 19) then observed:

> If such relationships are to become a reality in schools, there needs to be situations in which a multiplicity of voices, including those considered to be conflicting, are listened to and respected in equal measure to the more popular, conformist voices. The adults involved need to trust pupils' competencies and their abilities to offer insightful comments about a wide range of school-related issues, and to give serious consideration to the procedures around selecting whose voices are listened to, acknowledged and respected.

Engaging practice informed by 'counterpoint' could, in principle, create the conditions for different traditions of thinking to be engaged not only within research (rather than simply talking past one another), but also in situations of practice where, as in this situation, a greater hospitality to difference might be entertained.

(ii) Children's Rights and the Anthropology of the Good

The preceding discussion as regards a style of engagement links with a second theme in relation to imagined future trajectories for research in children's rights. An appeal to 'the good' has variously informed children's rights imaginaries and has been resolved in a number of different ways. This raises questions as to the kinds of ethical practice necessary if different forms of 'the good' are to be realised.

Such ethical questioning, linked to 'research on the cultural construction of the good', lies at the heart of a new movement within anthropology – the 'anthropology of the 'good' (Robbins, 2013, p. 457) – which is concerned both with teasing out different conceptions of the good that are implied, and with the specific forms of practices that are mobilised to this end. Given the importance of the 'good' to thinking and practice within the field of children's rights, engaging with this new tradition could provide rich resources for thinking differently and for exploring the ethical implications for mobilising rights in ways that go beyond the limitations of current translations into performance indicators. The scope of this work would also open research in children's rights to a broader range of traditions for thinking, beyond a more limited concern with western traditions and preoccupations. Such a tradition of thinking is future oriented and draws upon relational ontologies so as to explore 'the ways that people work on themselves so as to be able to realize the good in the creation of their moral selves'; to this extent, a focus is upon 'the ways people come to believe that they can successfully create a good beyond what is presently given in their lives' (Robbins, 2013, p. 458). There are a variety of different theoretical traditions engaged in this project, but the work of Faubian (2001, 2011), for example, draws upon the later ethical writings of Foucault (2005) as a means of exploring the different dimensions of this 'work on the self' in pursuit of the good.

(iii) Children's Rights and the Impact Agenda

Within the UK and elsewhere, there are increasing demands that researchers demonstrate 'impact' in relation to their research activities (e.g. ESRC, 2015). Recently, thinking in relation to the concept of impact has become more differentiated, distinguishing between, for example, conceptual, capacity building and instrumental impacts (ESRC, 2015). Such a categorisation potentially affords insights for thinking strategically about future developments within the field of research in children's rights, in so far as this focuses attention on broader academic and societal influence beyond the immediate concerns of a given project. This could be conceived as a provocation to engage framings that work beyond a limited instrumental conception that aims to take forward a particular theme to the exclusion of others, or beyond forms of research that are exclusively focused upon ontologies of the actual, rather than remaining open to the virtual (3. Iii, above). There are, in short, a number of ways in which attending to future impact might encourage practices that imagine otherwise. A politics of counterpoint and the anthropology of the good, as possible future trajectories, may likewise contribute to more inclusive and more generous styles of research in children's rights.

Concluding Remarks

The foregoing analysis has sought to identify a series of dominant tropes, tensions and productive ways forward in relation to research in children's rights. While there clearly are certain tensions within the field – that derive from issues of translation, different ontologies and different practice orientations – there is also evidence of a new theoretical vibrancy and inventiveness: a reaching out to make new connections and tackling the challenges that come from acknowledging limitations inherent in a limited concern with critique. To this extent, research work in children's rights and its multiple impacts are not settled but anticipatory; as such they might figure as *untimely* discourse, in Nietzsche's (1963, p. 60) sense, in so far as this acts 'counter to our time and thereby acting on our time and, let us hope, for the benefit of a time to come'.

Notes

[1] ECER Network 25 was inaugurated in 2003 with an explicit purpose to 'explore the ethical, methodological, legal and pedagogical issues that emerge at the intersection of children's rights and educational contexts. A particular focus is the ways in which children's rights provide a provocation to think and practice differently' (ECER, 2015).

[2] An illustration of such an approach can be found in the writings of the twelfth-century Islamic thinker Al-Ghazālī, that have recently been characterised as centred around a 'dialogic imagination' (see Moosa, 2005).

References

Allan, J., I'Anson, J., Fisher, S. & Priestley, A. (2005) *Promising Rights: introducing children's rights in school.* Edinburgh: Save the Children. https://www.savethechildren.org.uk/sites/default/files/docs/promising-rights(1)_1.pdf

Arneil, B. (2002) Becoming versus Being: a critical analysis of the child in liberal theory, in D. Archard & C.M. Macleod (Eds) *Moral and Political Status of Children*, pp. 70-96. Oxford: Oxford University Press.

Biesta, G.J.J. (2011) Disciplines and Theory in the Academic Study of Education: a comparative analysis of the Anglo-American and continental construction of the field, *Pedagogy, Culture and Society*, 19(2), 175-192. http://dx.doi.org/10.1080/14681366.2011.582255

Biesta, G.J.J. (2014) Traditions of Theory and Theorising in Education and their Significance for the Field of Children's Rights. Paper presented at Network 25, ECER, Porto, as contribution to paper session 'UNCRC and Traditions of Theorising'.

Brown, W. (2005) *Edgework: critical essays on knowledge and politics.* Princeton, NJ: Princeton University Press.

Candler, P.M. (2006) *Theology, Rhetoric, Manuduction.* London: SCM Press.

Clark, A. (2001) How to Listen to Very Young Children: the mosaic approach, *Childcare in Practice*, 7(4), 333-341. http://dx.doi.org/10.1080/13575270108415344

Colebrook, C. (2002) *Gilles Deleuze.* London: Routledge. http://dx.doi.org/10.4324/9780203241783

Coppock, V. (2002) Medicalising Children's Behaviour, in B. Franklin (Ed.) *The New Handbook of Children's Rights: comparative policy and practice*, 2nd edn, pp.139-154. London: Routledge.

Coppock, V. & McGovern, M. (2014) 'Dangerous Minds'? Deconstructing Counter-terrorism Discourse, Radicalisation and the 'Psychological Vulnerability' of Muslim Children and Young People in Britain, *Children and Society*, 28(3), 242-256. http://dx.doi.org/10.1111/chso.12060

Deleuze, G. (1988) *Bergsonism*, trans. H. Tomlinson & B. Habberjam. New York: Zone Books.

Depaepe, M. (1998) Educationalisation: a key concept in understanding the basic processes in the history of western education, *History of Education Review*, 27(1), 16-28.

Economic and Social Research Council (ESRC) (2015) What is Impact? http://www.esrc.ac.uk/research/evaluation-and-impact/what-is-impact/

Edwards, R. & Carmichael, P. (2012) Secret Codes: the hidden curriculum of semantic web technologies, *Discourse: Studies in the Cultural Politics of Education*, 33(4), 575-590. http://dx.doi.org/10.1080/01596306.2012.692963

European Conference on Educational Research (ECER) (2015) Research on Children's Rights in Education (Network 25). http://www.eera-ecer.de/networks/network25/

Evans, T. (2005) International Human Rights Law as Power/Knowledge, *Human Rights Quarterly*, 27(3), 1046-1068. http://dx.doi.org/10.1353/hrq.2005.0035

Faubion, J.D. (2001) Toward an Anthropology of Ethics: Foucault and the pedagogies of autopoiesis, *Representations*, 74(1), 83-104. http://dx.doi.org/10.1525/rep.2001.74.1.83

Faubion, J.D. (2011) *An Anthropology of Ethics*. Cambridge: Cambridge University Press. http://dx.doi.org/10.1017/CBO9780511792557

Fenwick, T., Edwards, R. & Sawchuck, P. (2011) *Emerging Approaches to Educational Research: tracing the socio-material*. London: Routledge.

Fenwick, T. & Landri, P. (2014) *Materialities, Textures and Pedagogies*. London: Routledge.

Foucault, M. (2005) *The Hermeneutics of the Subject: lectures at the College de France 1981-1982*, ed. F. Gros. New York: Palgrave Macmillan.

Francia, G. (2013) The Impacts of Individualization on Equity Educational Policies, *Journal of New Approaches to Educational Research*, 2(1), 17-22. http://dx.doi.org/10.7821/naer.2.1.17-22

Gilligan, C. (1982) *In a Different Voice*. Cambridge, MA: Harvard University Press.

Griffiths, A. & Kandel, R.F. (2000) Legislating for the Child's Voice: perspectives from comparative ethnography of proceedings involving children, in M. Maclean (Ed.) *Making Law for Families*, pp. 161-184. Oxford: Hart.

Hägglund, S. & Thelander, N. (2011) Children's Rights at 21: policy, theory, practice, *Education Inquiry*, 2(3), 365-372. http://dx.doi.org/10.3402/edui.v2i3.21988

Harcourt, D. (2011) An Encounter with Children: seeking meaning and understanding about childhood, *European Early Childhood Journal*, 19(3), 331-343. http://dx.doi.org/10.1080/1350293X.2011.597965

Harcourt, D. & Hägglund, S. (2013) Turning the UNCRC Upside Down: a bottom-up perspective on children's rights, *International Journal of Early Years Education*, 21(4), 286-299. http://dx.doi.org/10.1080/09669760.2013.867167

Holt, L. (Ed.) (2011) *Geographies of Children, Youth and Families: an international perspective*. Abingdon: Routledge.

I'Anson, J. (2011) Childhood, Complexity Orientation and Children's Rights: enlarging the space of the possible?, *Education Inquiry*, 2(3), 373-384.

I'Anson, J. (2013) Beyond the Child's Voice: towards an ethics for children's participation rights, *Global Studies of Childhood*, 3(2), 104-114. http://dx.doi.org/10.2304/gsch.2013.3.2.104

Ingold, T. (2003) Two Reflections on Ecological Knowledge, in G. Sanga & G. Ortalli (Eds) *Nature Knowledge: ethnoscience, cognition, identity*, pp. 301-311. New York: Berghahn.

Ingold, T. (2011) *Being Alive. Essays on Movement, Knowledge and Description*. London: Routledge.

James, A. (2007) Giving Voice to Children's Voices: practices and problems, pitfalls and potentials, *American Anthropologist*, 109(2), 261-272. http://dx.doi.org/10.1525/aa.2007.109.2.261

James, A., Jenks, C. & Prout, A. (1998) *Theorising Childhood*. Cambridge: Polity Press.

James, A. & Prout, A. (1997) *Constructing and Reconstructing Childhood: contemporary issues in the sociological study of childhood*. London: Routledge.

Jenks, C. (Ed.) (1982) *Sociology of Childhood: essential readings*. London: Batsford Academic and Educational.

Knorr Cetina, K. (1999) *Epistemic Cultures: how the sciences make knowledge*. Cambridge, MA: Harvard University Press.

Latour, B. (2004) Why Has Critique Run Out of Steam? From Matters of Fact to Matters of Concern, *Critical Inquiry* 30, 225-248. http://dx.doi.org/10.1086/421123

Latour, B. (2013) *An Investigation into the Modes of Existence: an anthropology of the moderns*. Cambridge, MA: Harvard University Press.

Lúcio, J. & I'Anson, J. (2015) Children as Members of a Community: citizenship, participation and educational development, *European Educational Research Journal*, 14, 129-137. http://dx.doi.org/10.1177/1474904115571794

Mannion, G. (2012) Intergenerational Education: the significance of 'reciprocity' and 'place', *Journal of Intergenerational Relations*, 10(4), 386-399. http://dx.doi.org/10.1080/15350770.2012.726601

Mannion, G. & Gilbert, J. (2015) Place-responsive Intergenerational Education, in R. Vanderbeck & N. Worth (Eds) *Intergenerational Space*, pp. 228-241. London: Routledge.

Mannion, G. & I'Anson, J. (2004) Beyond the Disneyesque: children's participation, spatiality and adult-child relations, *Childhood*, 11(3), 303-318.

Mannion, G., Sowerby, M. & I'Anson, J. (2015) *How Young People's Participation in School Supports Achievement and Attainment*. Scotland's Commissioner for Children & Young People (SCCYP).

Mayall, B. (2012) An Afterword: some reflections on a seminar series, *Children's Geographies*, 10(3), 347-355. http://dx.doi.org/10.1080/14733285.2012.693383

Moosa, E. (2005) *Ghazālī and the Poetics of Imagination*. Chapel Hill, NC: University of North Carolina Press.

Morrow, V. (1999) 'We Are People Too': children's and young people's perspectives on children's rights and decision-making in England, *International Journal of Children's Rights*, 7, 149-170. http://dx.doi.org/10.1163/15718189920494318

Nietzsche, F. (1963) On the Uses and Disadvantages of History for Life, in *Untimely Meditations*, trans. R.J. Hollingdale. Cambridge: Cambridge University Press.

Nussbaum, M. & Sen, A. (1999) *The Quality of Life*. Oxford: Clarendon Press.

Öman, M. & Quennerstedt, A. (2015) Questioning the No-touch Discourse in Physical Education from a Children's Rights Perspective, *Sport, Education and Society*, 1-16. http://dx.doi.org/10.1080/13573322.2015.1030384

Power, M. (1999) *The Audit Society: rituals of verification*. Oxford: Oxford University Press. http://dx.doi.org/10.1093/acprof:oso/9780198296034.001.0001

Quennerstedt, A. (2011) The Political Construction of Children's Rights in Education: a comparative analysis of Sweden and New Zealand, *Education Inquiry*, 2(3), 453-471. http://dx.doi.org/10.3402/edui.v2i3.21994

Quennerstedt, A. (2013) Children's Rights Research Moving into the Future: challenges on the way forward, *International Journal of Children's Rights*, 21(2), 233-247. http://dx.doi.org/10.1163/15718182-02102006

Qvortrup, J., Bardy, M., Sgritta, G. & Wintersberger, H. (Eds) (1994) *Childhood Matters. Social Theory, Practice and Politics*. Aldershot: Avebury.

Ranson, S. (2003) Public Accountability in the Age of Neo-liberal Governance, *Journal of Education Policy*, 18(5), 459-480. http://dx.doi.org/10.1080/0268093032000124848

Reynaert, D., Bouverne-De Bie, M. & Vandevelde, S. (2012) Between 'Believers' and 'Opponents': critical discussions on children's rights, *International Journal of Children's Rights*, 20(1), 155-168. http://dx.doi.org/10.1163/157181812X626417

Reynaert, D., De Bie, M. &Vandevelde, S. (2009) A Review of Children's Rights Literature since the Adoption of the United Nations Convention on the Rights of the Child, *Childhood*, 16(4), 518-534. http://dx.doi.org/10.1177/0907568209344270

Robbins, J. (2013) Beyond the Suffering Subject: toward an anthropology of the good, *Journal of the Royal Anthropological Institute*, New Series, 19, 447-462.

Robinson, C. (2013) Student Voice as a Contested Practice: power and participation in two student voice projects, *Improving Schools*, 16(1), 32-46. http://dx.doi.org/10.1177/1365480212469713

Robinson, C. (2014a) Children, Their Voices and Their Experiences of School: what does the evidence tell us? A Report for the Cambridge Primary Review Trust.

Robinson, C. (2014b) Developing Mutually Respectful Adult-child Relationships in Schools: is this a reality experienced equally by all pupils?, *Research Intelligence*, 125, 18-19.

Sachs, J. (2003) *The Activist Teaching Professional*. Buckingham: Open University Press.

Sargeant, J. & Harcourt, D. (2012) *Doing Ethical Research with Children*. Maidenhead: Open University Press.

Sebba, J. & Robinson, C. (2010) Evaluation of UNICEF UK's Rights Respecting Schools Award. Final Report. London: United Nations Children's Emergency Fund (UNICEF).

Sorensen, E. (2011) *The Materiality of Learning: technology and knowledge in educational practice*. Cambridge: Cambridge University Press.

Stammers, N. (1999) Social Movements and the Social Construction of Human Rights, *Human Rights Quarterly*, 21(4), 980-1008. http://dx.doi.org/10.1353/hrq.1999.0054

Strathern, M. (Ed.) (2000) *Audit Cultures: anthropological studies in accountability, ethics and the academy*. Abingdon: Routledge. http://dx.doi.org/10.4324/9780203449721

Thede, N. (2001) Human Rights and Statistics: some reflections on the no-man's-land between concept and indicator, *Statistical Journal of the United Nations Economic Commission for Europe*, 18(2/3), 259-273.

Thelander, N. (2009) 'We Are All the Same, But...' Kenyan and Swedish School Children's Views on Children's Rights. Dissertation, Karlstad University Studies.

Thrift, N. (2004) Summoning Life, in P. Cloke, P. Crang & M. Goodwin (Eds) *Envisioning Human Geographies*, pp. 81-103. London: Arnold.

Tisdall, E.K.M. & Punch, S. (2012) Not So 'New'? Looking Critically at Childhood Studies, *Children's Geographies*, 10(3), 249-264. http://dx.doi.org/10.1080/14733285.2012.693376

UK Government (2008) The United Nations Convention on the Rights of the Child: how legislation underpins implementation in England. https://www.gov.uk/government/uploads/system/uploads/attachment_data/file/296368/uncrc_how_legislation_underpins_implementation_in_england_march_2010.pdf

United Nations (1989) The United Nations Convention on the Rights of the Child (UNCRC), General Assembly resolution 44/25, 20 Nov. 1989. U.N. Doc. A/RES/44/25. http://www.ohchr.org/en/professionalinterest/pages/crc.aspx

Valentin, K. & Meinert, L. (2009) The Adult North and the Young South: reflections on the civilizing mission of children's rights, *Anthropology Today*, 25(3), 23-28. http://dx.doi.org/10.1111/j.1467-8322.2009.00669.x

Van Bueren, G. (2011) Multigenerational Citizenship: the importance of recognizing children as national and international citizens, *Annals of the American Academy of Political and Social Science*, 633(1), 30-51. http://dx.doi.org/10.1177/0002716210383113

CHAPTER 2

Educating Children and Young People on the UNCRC: actions, avoidance and awakenings

LOUISE GWENNETH PHILLIPS

SUMMARY Article 42 of the CRC asserts that 'States Parties undertake to make the principles and provisions of the Convention widely known, by appropriate and active means, to adults and children alike'. Yet since the ratification of the CRC in 1989, the CRC is not widely known to children and adults. Public discourses of children and childhood are considered as key hindrances to widespread promotion of the CRC. Significant actions that have taken place since 1989 to promote the CRC internationally and nationally are mapped, noting gaps, missed opportunities and possible explanations for neglect in the promotion of the CRC. To move forward in honouring children's rights through the CRC being widely known, possible awakenings in practice and policy are proposed.

Following the horrifying scale of human rights violation of WWII, the United Nations formulated the Declaration of Human Rights (UDHR) (United Nations General Assembly, 1948) based on the hope that awareness and practice of human rights would prevent the world suffering another holocaust (Gerber, 2013). The writers of the international legal instrument saw education as the key vehicle to cultivate awareness and practice of human rights, as stated in Article 26:

> Education shall be directed to the full development of the human personality and to the strengthening of respect for human rights and fundamental freedoms. It shall promote understanding, tolerance and friendship among all nations, racial or religious groups, and shall further the activities of the United Nations for the maintenance of peace. (United Nations General Assembly, 1948)

However, after more than sixty-five years of mandating and promoting human rights education (HRE) in the UDHR, international studies such as Gerber's (2008) study of schools in Melbourne, Australia and Boston, USA, and Lapayese's (2005) survey of HRE in secondary schools in Japan, Austria and the USA highlight that the implementation of HRE has been small and localised or that, if embedded at policy level, the implementation in classrooms is limited and weak.

The Convention on the Rights of the Child (CRC) (United Nations General Assembly, 1989) further enhanced the project for human rights-based education through promoting four key principles to a rights-based approach: 'non-discrimination, the best interests of the child, the optimum development of the child, and the right to express views' (UNICEF/UNESCO, 2007, p. 44). Article 42 of the CRC seeks to ensure that the Convention is public knowledge by declaring: 'States Parties undertake to make the principles and provisions of the Convention widely known, by appropriate and active means, to adults and children alike'.

Educated adults can readily access the Convention and many courses in law, education, policy and social welfare address the Convention. Yet, children's knowledge of their rights remains a largely unaddressed component of the Convention. For the enactment of rights, people need to know their rights, so they can deservedly claim their rights. A child cannot be a rights holder if they know not what rights they hold. Learning about rights builds an intrinsic sense of self-value and self-esteem (Feinberg, 1973). Children need to see themselves as having value not for any particular characteristics but purely for their existence. This chapter thereby explores the fulfilment of Article 42 since the ratification of the CRC in 1989 as an endeavour for the human rights education project.

Human rights are intergenerational, yet as Freeman (1994) attests, 'there can be no doubt that children are among the most vulnerable and powerless members of our societies today' (p. 307). Children are one of the last groups to claim rights, yet, unlike other marginalised groups, it is largely others (child advocates) claiming on children's behalf. The first step is for children to know their rights. Signatories to the Convention on the Rights of the Child are obligated to publicly promote the CRC. The Committee on the Rights of the Child requires signatory states to report on actions to address children's rights education in the first two years of becoming a signatory, then every five years from then on (Child Rights Connect, n.d.). Unfortunately, even with the international imperatives of the UDHR, CRC and regular reporting mechanisms, not all children know their rights, and I would even confidently suggest that the number of children who know their rights is minimal. Like McGowan (2012), I justify children's knowledge of their rights for both status-based and instrumental reasons. Each child's inherent dignity informs the status-based reason. Knowing, understanding and enacting children's rights provides the instrumental reasons that produce positive consequences, such as children feeling valued and in turn flourishing, causing intergenerational civic engagement to prosper.

To understand influences on the promotion of CRC to children, dominant conceptualisations of social constructs of children and childhood are discussed. A mapping of international, national and NGO endeavours to make the CRC widely known to children follows. The range of endeavours discussed is by no means definitive, but rather plots some significant contributors to the Article 42 project. References to endeavours in each continent have been sourced, to reflect a global sketch of the actions taken. Yet, as an English-speaking Australian author, content on actions was limited to publications in English, and national actions are more Australian-centric as this is the context I know best. What I provide is by no means definitive or comprehensive, but rather a broad brushstroke view of the global landscape of what is happening to promote the CRC to children in international programs and national initiatives. To conclude, I will explore possible future directions as necessary awakenings for children to be and act as rights holders and claimers in all facets of society across the globe.

Public Discourse on Children's Rights

To understand why there has been minimal uptake of public promotion of the CRC to children, the following discusses a range of conceptions of children and childhood. Both historical and contemporary constructions of the child as unruly, as immanent, as innocent, as developing and as a social actor are explained. All constructions continue to be in circulation.

Historically, in societies children have little, if any, status. They are typically seen as the property of their parents or guardians, which originated from Roman law and has largely remained (see Archard, 2015), and as under the rule of teachers and schools, so that children are deprived of rights and treated any way their 'owners' see fit. The Christian Old Testament and the theories of philosopher Thomas Hobbes (1660/1996) argued for total parental dominion over children, who were understood as unruly, requiring adults to beat the wildness out through discipline and control. This way of thinking informed the establishment of schools (Luke, 1989), with the expectation that through sustained discipline, over time children would become good adult citizens who follow the social order (James et al, 1998). Violent disciplining of children continues to be permissible in schools in 98 nation states across the world (Global Initiative to End All Corporal Punishment of Children, 2015). Other factors, such as the standardisation of curricular content and rules, also limit scope for children to make decisions and express opinions. Together, these factors of discipline and control insist on obedience and deprive children of their rights.

A view of a child as immanent (or a blank slate) informed by the tabula rasa thesis espoused by John Locke (Locke, 1690/1959) also supports a rightsless status for children. This is especially the case in status-based justifications based on the ability of rational thought. Reason is understood as being acquired with age, thus defining children as becoming or latent reasoners. Based on this view, adults have a higher status and exercise control over children because of age, experience and knowledge. Social policy in western societies perpetuates such a view by largely defining children and young people as 'incompetents' (Morrow, 1994, p. 51). The enactment of children as immanent sees children removed from responsibility, and reliant on adults for care, protection and education. Children's exclusion from various social practices and responsibilities, based on the perception of their inherent incompetence, drastically reduces opportunity for their participation rights.

Conceptions of children as angelic, uncorrupted by the world, and naturally good, as espoused by Rousseau (Rousseau, 1762/2007), inform a view of children as innocent. To Rousseau, children were born with a natural goodness. On the basis of this understanding, adults 'generate a desire to shelter children from the corrupt surrounding world' (Dahlberg et al, 1999, p. 45). Adults seek to maintain the natural goodness of children by protecting them from violence and corruption through surveillance, limitation, regulation and withholding knowledge. Such restraints create children who feel vulnerable and disempowered, reinforcing notions of child as ignorant or immanent (e.g. see Cannella & Viruru, 2004). As Dahlberg et al (1999) claimed, by protecting children from the world, adults do not respect the rights and capabilities of children to seriously engage in the world. A view of children as innocent dominates the implementation of the CRC, seeing widespread discourses of protection place emphasis on protection rights (James et al, 2008; Archard, 2015) rather than welcome children's participation rights (e.g. access to information, freedom of thought and association, expression of opinions, and decision-making).

Empirical research conducted by Piaget (e.g. see 1932) in which he determined that there is a developmental pathway to intelligence shaped a view of children as developing. Such a view positions adults as competent and supreme, and children as incomplete, incompetent and irrational as a result of their developing status (James et al, 1998). Viewing children as in preparation for future participation (not agential in the present) masks the extent to which children are capable and undertake responsibility in their lives. The positioning of adults as competent and capable beings who understand, translate and interpret children's comments and actions (Waksler, 1991) sees knowledge of children's rights being simplified and shared at stages when an adult deems the child is developmentally ready to understand.

More recently, there has been growing sociological interest in and attention to children and childhood. Sociological understandings acknowledge children as agential, with 'social, political and economic status as contemporary subjects' (James et al, 1998, p. 26) – that is, as rights holders and claimers of today.

In modern times, two key books, *Birthrights* (Farson, 1974) and *Escape from Childhood* (Holt, 1975), forged a children's liberation movement arguing for self-determination for children, so that they have the same rights as adults. Both authors positioned children as one of the major oppressed groups in western society, with families and schools as major sources of oppression for children. In the CRC, 'children are not accorded the same self-determination rights as adults' (McGowan, 2012, p. 74), due to their economic dependency and reduced access to civic institutions (James et al, 2008; Millei & Imre, 2009).

In opposition to the child liberationists are those who argue a caretaker thesis for children, which denies self-determination for children, because self-determination is deemed too important to be in the hands of children (Archard, 2015). Commitment to the caretaker thesis is informed by conceptions of children as innocent, immanent and developing, in that they are vulnerable, requiring protection, and have not yet developed the cognitive capacity for self-determination. Since the ratification of the CRC in 1989, the United Nations (UN), national, state and local governments and non-governmental organisations (NGOs) have primarily focused on legislation, policies, action plans and reports to ensure children's rights to life, health, education and welfare. Yet, Farson (1974) would argue that such actions have been about protecting children, not their rights. As Archard (2015) explains, 'it is consonant with a paternalistic view of children as needing adults to secure their welfare' (p. 66). Child liberationists seek for children to choose and act themselves in their health, education and welfare rights. The caretaker thesis has dominated the implementation of the CRC – perhaps because it 'has a pleasing concordant completeness. A child is denied the right of self-determination in order that s/he should able to exercise that right in adulthood' (Archard, 2015, p. 75). For example, by denying a child the right to choose schooling or not, the child will then acquire necessary knowledge for reflective thought for self-determination.

Collectively, the above discussion captures a range of conceptions of children and childhood in public discourses that are shaping the implementation and promotion of the CRC. Historical constructions of children and childhood remain entrenched in public discourse, so that conceptions of children as unruly, immanent, innocent and developing continue to restrict and restrain fulfilment of children as rights holders and claimers, and paternalistic enactment of the CRC is maintained. The following sections will provide an overview of international and national programmes to promote children's rights to children, with consideration of how conceptions of children enable and constrain children's capacity to flourish as rights holders.

International Programmes for Children to Know Their Rights

The United Nations and NGOs have played the most significant roles in the various initiatives enacted across the globe to promote the CRC since its ratification in 1989. To provide a sense of how social, political and cultural trends have influenced initiatives, they are discussed roughly in chronological order of their commencement, starting with the UNICEF Child Friendly Schools, then the UNICEF Rights Respecting schools in the UK and Canada, followed by the United Nations World Programme for Human Rights Education.

UNICEF Child Friendly Schools

Child Friendly Schools first developed in Thailand in 1997 (UNICEF, 2006), inspired by the principles of the CRC (UNICEF, 2009), and can be 'understood to be a microcosm of a society, where the social, cultural, economic, and political dynamics, including ethnolinguistic tensions, of nations and communities interact, collide, and are addressed through a rights-based approach' (Clair et al, 2012, p. 6). Motivated by children's right to education and the honouring of children as rights holders, the schools are established in areas where children do not have access to schooling. UNICEF developed the concept of Child Friendly Schools in recognition that single-factor approaches (e.g. resource materials or professional development) produced short-lived gains, so they looked to a whole-package approach to improving the quality of education. By 2007, Child Friendly Schools existed in 56 countries (UNICEF, 2009).

After the division of the Soviet Union and Yugoslavia, several countries in Central Eastern Europe experienced political instability, economic collapse and destruction of social services, so that countries such as Turkey, Macedonia and Azerbaijan looked to the international framework of Child Friendly Schools to improve their education systems in the 2000s. Clair et al (2012) found in their assessment of Child Friendly Schools in Central Eastern Europe that the schools usually include dimensions of: inclusiveness; effectiveness; a healthy, safe and protective learning environment; democratic participation; and equal opportunities regardless of gender. Children have a say in the form and substance of their education, enacting democratic participation.

A great example of children's democratic participation in Child Friendly Schools can be found in the child governments at Child Friendly Schools in Mali. The children participate in a two-month training course on child rights and Child Friendly Schools. They then analyse their school according to children's rights to choose areas in need of attention, form committees (with students from all grades) for each identified problem area and elect ministers, half of whom must be girls (UNICEF, 2009). The strategy rapidly spread across Mali schools and is now a nationally approved strategy by the Ministry of Education in Mali. Child governments provide children with knowledge of their rights and awareness that 'these rights have practical implications for themselves, their schools and their communities' (UNICEF, 2009, Chapter 5, p. 28). Such accounts of this initiative appear to reflect a construction of children as social actors, though the only source located is from UNICEF, which characteristically presents its programmes positively.

Child Friendly Schools continue to be established in countries in every continent. UNICEF actively promotes its Child Friendly Schools as models of quality practice to inform national education systems. Clair et al (2012) claim that 'observational and anecdotal data suggest that children are learning about their rights' (p. 19), offering 'a promising approach to improving educational quality and enhancing equity that is both school-based and system-focused' (p. 7). However, UNICEF recognises that 'there has been a tendency to overprescribe on Child Friendly Schools and to underemphasize training and capacity for using the CFS model in education systems' (p. 7). This suggests that the name and concept is often readily seized without adequate understanding of the right-based theoretical underpinnings. Regardless, there are thousands of Child Friendly Schools across the globe with overt embedded practices, making children's rights known to children in underprivileged nations, in what appears to be a vision of children as social actors of today.

UNICEF Rights Respecting Schools in the UK and Canada

In economically rich nations, such as the UK and Canada, in collaboration with UNICEF, schools that wish to embrace rights-respecting practice and ethos have sought to be certified as rights respecting. Referred to as Rights Respecting Schools, they teach, promote and respect children's rights (according to the CRC) and create everyday opportunities for students to practise their rights in classrooms, schools and communities.

The initiative began in the UK in 2004, and has played a significant role in the promotion of children's rights throughout the UK (Sebba & Robinson, 2010). To be awarded as a Rights Respecting School, schools are required to demonstrate the following four evidence-based standards:

– Rights-respecting values underpin leadership and
   management;

- The whole school community learns about the UN Convention on the Rights of the Child;
- The school has a rights-respecting ethos;
- Children are empowered to become active learners and citizens (UNICEF UK, n.d, p. 4).

There are three levels to progress through, from recognition of commitment to level 2, which can take up to four years to achieve. Interest in and commitment to the initiative has consistently grown over the years, with over 3200 primary, secondary and special schools registered for the award in England, Northern Ireland, Scotland and Wales in 2014 (Robinson, 2014a).

UNICEF Canada commenced the Rights Respecting School initiative in 2007, drawing from the UK Rights Respecting Schools Award (RRSA) with adaptation to the Canadian context. A 'Rights Respecting School involves placing the Convention at the heart of the school's culture' (UNICEF Canada, 2011, p. 3) and is based on four building blocks:

- Awareness for the whole school community of the CRC;
- Student participation in school community through sharing opinions and making decisions;
- Teaching and learning rights-respecting practice and responsibilities;
- Children's rights inform policies, programme choices and implementation.

The process of becoming a Rights Respecting School in Canada can take two to three years (UNICEF Canada, 2011).

Following a three-year evaluation (2007-2010) of UNICEF UK's Rights Respecting Schools Award, Sebba and Robinson (2010) found that across the 31 schools evaluated, rights and responsibilities were made explicit in lessons, assemblies, displays and most often in peer interaction and conflict resolution. Children in roles as Pupil Improvement Partners and RRSA ambassadors were also endorsed to promote knowledge and application of the rights of the child. Robinson (2014a) also noticed a slackening of more rigid hierarchical power relations which have dominated school relationships, and a move towards adults and school staff engaging in more deliberate dialogue about school-related issues with children and young people. As a consequence of rights education and rights-respecting practice, Robinson found that pupils reported 'a greater enjoyment of school, classroom conditions more conducive to learning, positive attitudes towards diversity, a reduction in bullying and, where there were conflicts, pupils were more likely to resolve these themselves' (p. 18). Yet, it is important to acknowledge that amid these positive gains for children enrolled in Rights Respecting Schools, Robinson (2014b) identified two major concerns on how rights respecting these schools truly are for all children.

Her first concern was that though the students made decisions about school-related issues, the nature of these issues was not central to the school; instead they were minor peripheral issues of little consequence. The relinquishing of adult control thus only occurred for matters that were inconsequential to the operation of the school. The second concern was that rights-respecting practices focused on students who agreed with what the adults in the school wanted to hear, as opposed to those whose views countered the school values, thus suggesting that there were conditions placed on children's rights.

Though there are great social and political gains for children in Rights Respecting Schools, it seems that the shackles of discipline and control that have ruled schools for centuries have only slightly loosened, to maintain adult control of what children make decisions about, and to listen to children only if they say what teachers want to hear. It is also unsettling that UNICEF runs two different school programmes to implement the CRC, one for developing (or post-conflict) countries and another for developed nations, with differing names. Is 'child friendly' the diminutive of 'rights respecting', perhaps unwittingly continuing global north paternalism? Clair et al (2012) also acknowledge the light nature of the label and its poor capacity to translate well into other languages.

World Programme for Human Rights Education – First Phase

Following the 1989 ratification of the CRC, NGOs like UNICEF and Save the Children have carried the main role in provisioning children's rights education resources. The World Conference on Human Rights in Vienna in 1993 noted little achievement in promoting human rights education (HRE) since the adoption of the UNDHR in 1948, thus declaring 1995-2004 the Decade of Human Rights Education. The value of human rights education was defined as 'essential for the promotion and achievement of stable and harmonious relations among communities and for fostering mutual understanding, tolerance and peace' (World Conference on Human Rights, 1993, p. 25). Within this HRE decade, UNESCO developed a 'Plan of Action: world programme for human rights education', Phase 1: 2005-2007 [1] (UNESCO, 2006) to guide efforts for improved implementation of human rights education in member states. The first phase of the world programme specifically aimed 'to promote the inclusion and practice of human rights in the primary and secondary school systems' (UNESCO, 2006, p. 20).

The first phase (2005-2007) of the World Programme for Human Rights Education (WPHRE) encouraged member states to undertake, as a minimum, stages 1 *(analyse the situation of HRE in the school system)* and 2 *(develop a national implementation strategy)* and initiate stage 3 *(implement and monitor activities)*. Unfortunately, many member states did not meet these stages within the first phase time frame (2005-2007), seeing an extension to 2009. Yet still little progress occurred, and to date only 19 member states (and none of these are English-speaking nations) have submitted national action plans for human rights education to the UN Office of the High Commissioner for Human Rights (Office of the High Commissioner for Human Rights, 2015). For example, in Australia in 2009 the Human Rights Commission noted that:

> – In Australia, there is no cohesive approach by state and
> territory education departments to the delivery of human
> rights education at the primary and secondary levels …
> – There is also a lack of professional development and support
> for educators (across all curriculum areas) who teach human
> rights content …
> – In order to fulfil the goals of the WPHRE, the Commission
> has recommended to DEEWR [Department of Education,
> Employment and Workplace Relations] that there be an audit
> (situational analysis) of all of the human rights education
> initiatives that currently exist in Australian education systems.
> This has not occurred to date (Australian Human Rights
> Commission, 2009, p. 3).

When writing this chapter in December 2015, little had progressed in these three areas, aside from attention being given to teaching about and through human rights in the general capability of *ethical understanding* in the new national curriculum (more about this in the national curricula section later) and, in 2012, the first phase of a situational analysis of HRE in Australian schooling being funded and undertaken (see Burridge et al, 2013); the second phase was to examine HRE in practice, but the incoming conservative federal government cut the funding.

Though the first phase of the world programme focused on HRE in primary and secondary schools and explicitly drew on the principles of the CRC, only teachers and school staff are referred to as rights holders in the document, not children and young people. Specific attention to education staff and parents as rights holders was also noted in many UNICEF documents, notably to address arguments against children's rights, in which adults fear that giving power to children and young people will result in reduced rights for adults (e.g. see Howe & Covell, 2005). However, evaluations of rights-based schools demonstrate that HRE enhances relationships between staff and students (Covell & Howe, 2008; Sebba & Robinson, 2010).

The world programme has brought greater global attention to HRE, with Tibbitts and Fernekes (2011) noting a significant increase in HRE resources, programmes and the embedding of HRE in national curricula since the launching of the world programme in 2005. Though the world programme addresses the broader umbrella of HRE, knowledge of the CRC is included; to what degree varies by nation, as discussed next.

National Initiatives

The following describes key national initiatives for children to know their rights. The three main avenues identified in a review of literature, reports and online media are: national curricula and policy; children's commissioners; and media programmes. Once again, please note this is by no means a comprehensive coverage of national initiatives globally, but rather provides a sketch of key themes at play in national initiatives to educate children and young people on their rights.

National Curricula and Policy for Children and Young People

The UN Committee on the Rights of the Child states: 'Children do not lose their human rights by virtue of passing through the school gates' (2001). However, as institutions of discipline and control, many schools do not honour children's rights, or do so only in limited, tokenistic ways. Many human rights education scholars and advocates, such as Fernekes (1992) and Tibbitts (2002, 2009), have argued for explicitly embedding the teaching of rights in curricula to build awareness of international human rights legal instruments to create greater social harmony. In 1992, Fernekes noted that since the 1980s most social studies curricula have overlooked or addressed in a very minimal way children's rights, especially as they are defined in the CRC. As this was only three years after the CRC was ratified, you may consider this understandable. However, now, more than 25 years since the CRC was ratified, the situation remains largely the same.

The Centre for Children's Rights, Queen's University, Belfast recently led an investigation of the implementation by 12 countries (Australia, Belgium, Canada, Denmark, Germany, Iceland, Ireland, New Zealand, Norway, South Africa, Spain and Sweden) of the UNCRC (Lundy et al, 2012). They found that few interviewees (aside from Norway's) identified children's rights education as important in the implementation of the UNCRC. Most countries did include aspects of human rights and child rights in their school curricula, yet rarely in extensive ways to achieve any influence as the inclusion was only optional. For example, in examination of education policy in Sweden and New Zealand, Quennerstedt (2011) noted children's knowledge about their rights is constructed as a minor issue in Sweden, only occasionally mentioned and never thoroughly discussed, whilst it is not raised at all in New Zealand policy. Ramirez et al's (2006) investigation of the growth of human rights education worldwide found that nations with a history of human rights abuses were slightly more likely to include HRE in curricula, and this was further increased if they had international linkages to the broader human rights movement. For example, the post-apartheid South African curriculum ensures that all learning areas reflect respect for human rights; however, Keet and Carrim (2006) question the politics at play, with the curriculum playing a symbolic role in marking the distinct move from apartheid to post-apartheid.

The perception that rights education is seen as political provides a strong rationale for the minimal uptake of embedding children's rights education in curricula. Actions of inequality and injustice enacted by states can be questioned and challenged, potentially placing schools in opposition to the state, and hence we witness states excluding children's rights in curricula regardless of multiple international imperatives (i.e. UNDHR, CRC and the Word Programme for HRE). Rights education is often associated with Marxist or leftist agendas, so those schools that do employ rights education focus on content rather than advocacy (Tibbitts & Fernekes, 2011), what Tibbitts refers to as a values and awareness approach to HRE, whereas advocacy work follows a transformative approach (Tibbitts, 2002). Children's subservience, compliance, vulnerability and silence are maintained through active avoidance of children knowing their rights.

In early childhood curricula in Australia, it is a different story. For example, the Early Years Learning Framework for Australia (Commonwealth of Australia, 2009) specifically states, 'Early childhood educators guided by the Framework will reinforce in their daily practice the principles laid out in the United Nations Convention on the Rights of the Child (the Convention)' (p. 5). Attention to children's rights is woven throughout the document with a specified outcome dedicated to children knowing their rights. To further reinforce children's rights education in early childhood in Australia, the Australian Human Rights Commission and Early Childhood Australia (2015) have recently released the 'Supporting Young Children's Rights: statement of intent (2015-2018)' 'to guide professionals working with young children to support and advocate for young children's rights in their day-to-day practice' (p. 1). In this document, one of five key themes is engaged civics and citizenship, which explicitly addresses children being informed of their rights. Comparatively, the Australian Curriculum (version 8) (Australian Curriculum Assessment and Reporting Authority, 2015) for schools only mentions the CRC as a possible investigation in history and in civics and citizenship for year 10 in secondary school. Attention to understanding rights as a concept is explicitly defined in the general capacity of *ethical understanding*; however, no rights document is referred to to inform such learning. Those in the early childhood sector in Australia are noticeably stronger proponents for children's rights than those in the schooling sector. Perhaps it is considered less threatening to adult control for younger children to know their rights.

Schools seem to offer the ideal forum to address the international imperative of article 42 of the CRC, in that schooling is compulsory in most member states, maximising information to the broadest population of children across the world. Unfortunately, as the above brief summary of assessments of CRC in national curricula attests, the uptake has been minimal, suggesting deficit constructions of children (i.e. as unruly, immanent, innocent, developing) dominating curriculum development.

Children's Commissioners

One strategy to promote children's rights that member states have progressively adopted has been the appointment of a public representative to advocate for children. Norway was the first nation to appoint a public representative for children through the role of the Ombudsman for Children in 1981. Sweden followed with a Commissioner for Children established in 1985. Since then many other countries have followed: New Zealand in 1989, Wales in 2001, Northern Ireland in 2003, Scotland in 2004, England in 2005, and Australia in 2013.[2] Children's commissioners across the world have all contributed significantly to increasing children's knowledge and understanding of their rights through varying dissemination strategies (Boylan & Dalrymple, 2009).

In Australia, within two years of appointment, the national children's commissioner, Megan Mitchell (with her team), implemented a number of strategies to promote children's awareness of the CRC. These strategies have sought to rectify the United Nations Concluding Observations to Australia's report to the Committee on the Rights of the Child (2012): 'the Committee remains concerned that awareness and knowledge of the Convention continues to be limited amongst children, professionals working with or for children, and the general public' (p. 5). In 2013, the children's commissioner facilitated the *Big Banter* to consult with children across Australia both face to face and through online surveys. A major theme identified was children's and the general public's limited knowledge about children's rights (National Children's Commissioner, 2013). The following year the commissioner's office developed children's rights resources, child- and youth-friendly versions of her 2013 and 2014 children's rights reports, and child- and youth-friendly versions of the 2012 United Nations Committee on the Rights of the Child's Concluding Observations (National Children's Commissioner, 2014).

Children's commissioners have proven to play significant roles in the promotion of children's rights; however, their role often yields little political power. The powers they yield vary across nations but often have 'no executive authority, both legally and via instruction' (Boylan & Dalrymple, 2009, p. 29). They are appointed as public servants and so advise and provide information to the government of their nation.

Media Programs for Children's Rights

Another initiative to make the CRC well known to both children and adults involves public media programmes. Saunders and Goddard (2002, n.p.) claim that 'the constructive use of mass media can assist in teaching children and young people socially desirable ways of dealing with conflict, knowledge of their rights to integrity and protection from harm, healthy eating habits and lifestyles, and ways to assert themselves and their rights in a positive, acceptable manner'. Further, media scholars note that media for children and popular culture play a powerful role in children's shared culture and meaning-making (e.g. see Perry, 2013).

Perhaps the most well-known and longest-lasting media programme on children's rights is South Africa's Soul Buddyz, developed by the Soul City Institute (a South African non-governmental organisation that seeks to develop safe and healthy communities through mass media interventions) (Goldstein et al, 2001). It began distribution in 2000 for children (8-12-year-olds) to learn their rights in a way that had meaning with their own life experiences. The project consists of a television programme, a radio programme and supporting print material. To date there have been five series of the television programme from 2000 to 2011, each with 26 thirty-minute episodes with child actors facing rights issues in everyday life experiences, screened on South Africa's most popular channel. The radio programme provides similar content to the television series through radio plays, along with young people and experts hosting a talk show on rights issues. Throughout South Africa, year 7 students receive booklets (linked to the television programme) and three posters (with a game to assess whether rights were being infringed). Through newspapers and NGOs, parents receive a parenting booklet on how to communicate respectfully with children, building their self-esteem and supporting them through life's challenges.

To maintain public dialogue on children's rights issues and to be consultative with children and the community, the programme facilitates multiple strategies such as Soul Buddyz clubs in schools which aim to provide a platform that gives voice to, and promotes real action for, children's health and well-being, and regular community evaluations. The concept of Soul Buddyz clubs began in 2003, in response to children's requests, and they were set up through a partnership between the Soul City Institute, the South African Broadcasting Channel (SABC) Education (a national broadcaster channel) and the Department of Education (Schmid et al, 2010). By 2009, 5255 clubs existed, representing a quarter of South African primary schools, mostly in poor, rural under-resourced communities (Schmid et al, 2010). Facilitated by trained volunteer educators, the clubs are founded on 'principles of ongoing learning, child participation, children's rights and children as active and proactive citizens and agents of change' (Schmid et al, 2010, p. 274). In Schmid et al's evaluation of the successfulness of Soul Buddyz clubs, evidence demonstrated that 'children could advocate on behalf of themselves and could mobilise community members and institutions to ensure that school and community needs were being addressed' (p. 280). All facilitators of the clubs declared to Schmid et al that having children lead the process was central to each club's success. However, Schmid et al questioned the degree to which the clubs can be child-led when the programme is highly structured and monitored by the Soul City Institute. Widespread participation in the programme continues across South Africa (Soul City Institute, 2015).

The potential to promote the CRC to children and young people through media seems largely untapped. The Office of the Ombudsman for Children, Republic of Ireland launched in 2014 an iPad app called *It's Your Right* in an effort to tap into desirable new media platforms, though it is information based with limited interactivity. Appealing to young audiences requires innovative utilisation of the agency new media affords (Kalantzis & Cope, 2010) and connection with popular culture interests (Perry, 2013), with children's rights embedded into everyday stories with hooks of interest: the unusual, the fantastical, the risky, the adventurous.

Potential Awakenings for the UNCRC to be Widely Known to Children

The preceding discussion plotted actions that have taken place to make the CRC widely known to children. They have most significantly occurred through NGOs, with only a small percentage of children reached. There clearly are blocks, given that more than 25 years of this international imperative have passed. Commonly held deficit perceptions of children and childhood play a significant role in the hindrances and avoidance of CRC promotion and education, and many argue that progress has not happened in schools because children's rights education is scarce in teacher education and professional development. Potential ways forward for making the CRC widely known to children require shifts in attitude towards children, teacher education and innovative and creative utilisation of new media.

Many (e.g. UNESCO, 2006; Tibbitts & Fernekes, 2011; Burridge et al, 2013; Robinson, 2014a) recommend the need for: teacher education on rights education, and teachers already in the profession requiring comprehensive professional development. The World Programme for HRE (first phase) explicitly noted the stipulation of training for teachers in HRE in education policies to provide 'necessary knowledge, understanding, skills and competencies to facilitate the learning and practice of human rights in schools' (p. 19). Robinson (2014a) explains that 'new entrants to the profession need to be able to see the value of schools adopting a rights-respecting approach, and have an understanding about how to promote this work in schools' (p. 19). At present, the typical offering of human rights courses at universities is located in history, political and social sciences departments of universities, with little evidence of cross-disciplinary course work or study in HRE (Tibbitts & Fernekes, 2011). And Tibbitts (2002) points out that human rights training is typically provided by people who have had experience in human rights education; there is no standard of what defines a human rights education trainer. Further educational research into the knowledge and skills, values and attitudes, and actions employed in the teaching and learning of children and young people's rights in early childhood settings and schools is required to guide and inform HRE in teacher education. Education faculties need to collaborate with political and social science departments to develop and provide tuition on rights education courses that demonstrate rights as defined in UN instruments through experiential democratic processes, as recommended (e.g. see Lansdown, 2001; Howe & Covell, 2005; McGowan, 2012). Globally, at present, high-stakes assessment dominates schooling practice, policy and decision-making, which shifts attention to numbers rather than social gains. Evaluations (e.g. Covell & Howe, 2008) of children's rights education programmes list many learning outcomes, to play into the outcomes-based rhetoric of the present neo-liberal agenda. McGowan (2012) proposes that we look more broadly to 'the potential positive effect on the rest of society of the very existence of these "oases" of respect for rights' to offer 'a beacon of hope of what is possible in the present and the future' (p. 75) and that we should not feel obliged to demonstrate learning but rather that we honour children's rights on the basis of their inherent dignity.

Decision-makers will make teacher education and professional development in children's rights education happen when they see children as social actors, as citizens of today, as opposed to clinging to perceptions of children as unruly, innocent, incompetent and developing. The provocation for such an attitudinal shift can be enabled through first-hand experiences with children demonstrating their capabilities and competence as citizens of the world (e.g. see Hickey & Phillips, 2013; Phillips & Hickey, 2013; Phillips, 2014), so that the joy, curiosity, concerns and capabilities of being a child are heard, seen and felt.

Finally, to inform children of their rights, the broad range of information technology available needs to be tapped into. South Africa's Soul Buddyz multi-pronged programme offers a great example, though now we have many platforms to play with. New media provide readily accessible agency for children and young people to select the texts they view and create themselves (e.g. YouTube clips, memes, vines). The way children and young people utilise media needs to be carefully considered and embedded into CRC communication strategies in order to captivate them. Children already initiate and create texts on their lived experiences. Perhaps an online network of slightly older buddies, like the child government model in Mali (whose members have training on the CRC), can act to highlight honouring and denial of children's rights as comments or pop-ups on highly utilised platforms like YouTube and Facebook.

The way forward for children to be fully honoured as rights holders requires openness to children's ways of being, structural commitment to rights education and experiential creativity and innovation.

Notes

[1] To date there have been three phases to the World Programme for Human Rights Education: Phase 1, 2005-2007 (extended to 2009); Phase 2, 2010-2014; and Phase 3, 2015-2019.

[2] States and territories of Australia appointed children's commissioners earlier, the first being appointed for Queensland in 1996.

References

Archard, D. (2015) *Children Rights and Childhood*, 3rd edn. Abingdon: Routledge.

Australian Curriculum Assessment and Reporting Authority (2015) Australian Curriculum v8. http://www.australiancurriculum.edu.au/

Australian Human Rights Commission (2009) World Programme for Human Rights Education. Australian Human Rights Commission submission to the Office of the High Commissioner for Human Rights re possible focus for the second phase of the World Programme for Human Rights Education. https://www.humanrights.gov.au/sites/default/files/content/legal/submissio ns/2009/200907_WPHRE.pdf

Australian Human Rights Commission (2009) World Programme for Human Rights Education. Australian Human Rights Commission submission to the Office of the High Commissioner for Human Rights re: possible focus for the second phase of the World Programme for Human Rights Education Sydney: Australian Human Rights Commission.

Australian Human Rights Commission & Early Childhood Australia (2015) Supporting Young Children's Rights: statement of intent (2015-2018). https://http://www.humanrights.gov.au/sites/default/files/supporting_young _children_rights.pdf

Boylan, J. & Dalrymple, J. (2009) *Understanding Advocacy for Children and Young People*. Maidenhead: Open University Press.

Burridge, N., Chodkiewicz, A., Payne, A.M., Oguro, S., Varnham, S. & Buchanan, J. (2013) *Human Rights Education in the School Curriculum.* Sydney: Cosmopolitan Civil Societies Research Centre, University of Technology, Sydney.

Cannella, G.S. & Viruru, R. (2004) *Childhood and Postcolonization: power, education and contemporary practice,* New York: RoutledgeFalmer.

Child Rights Connect (n.d.) *The Reporting Cycle of the Committee on the Rights of the Child.* Geneva: Child Rights Connect.

Clair, N., Miske, S. & Patel, D. (2012) Child Rights and Quality Education. *European Education,* 44, 5-22. http://dx.doi.org/10.2753/EUE1056-4934440201

Commonwealth of Australia (2009) *Belonging, Being and Becoming: the early years learning framework for Australia.* Canberra: Australian Government Department of Education, Employment and Workplace Relations for the Council of Australian Governments.

Covell, K. & Howe, B. (2008) *Rights, Respect and Responsibility: final report on the County of Hampshire rights education initiative.* Nova Scotia: Cape Breton University.

Dahlberg, G., Moss, P. & Pence, A. (1999) *Beyond Quality in Early Childhood Education and Care: post-modern perspectives.* London: Falmer Press.

Farson, R. (1974) *Birthrights.* New York: Macmillan.

Feinberg, J. (1973) *Social Philosophy.* Englewood Cliffs, NJ: Prentice Hall.

Fernekes, W. (1992) Children's Rights in the Social Studies Curriculum: a critical imperative, *Social Education,* 56, 203-204.

Freeman, M. (1994) Whither Children: protection, participation, autonomy, *Manitoba Law Journal,* 22, 307-327.

Gerber, P. (2008) *From Convention to Classroom: the long road to human rights education.* Saarbrücken: VDM.

Gerber, P. (2013) *Understanding Human Rights: educational challenges for the future.* Cheltenham: Edward Elgar. http://dx.doi.org/10.4337/9781781006061

Global Initiative to End All Corporal Punishment of Children (2015) Global Progress towards Prohibiting All Corporal Punishment. http://www.endcorporalpunishment.org/assets/pdfs/legality-tables/Global progress table with terrs %28alphabetical%29.pdf

Goldstein, S., Anderson, A., Usdin, S. & Japhet, G. (2001) Soul Buddyz: a children's rights mass media campaign in South Africa, *Health and Human Rights,* 5, 163-173. http://dx.doi.org/10.2307/4065370

Hickey, A. & Phillips, L. (2013) New Kids on the Block: young people, the city and public pedagogies, *Global Studies of Childhood,* 3, 115-128. http://dx.doi.org/10.2304/gsch.2013.3.2.115

Hobbes, T. (1660/1996) *The Leviathan.* New York: Oxford University Press.

Holt, J. (1975) *Escape from Childhood: the needs and rights of children,* Harmondsworth: Penguin.

Howe, R.B. & Covell, K. (2005) *Empowering Children: Children's rights education as a pathway to citizenship,* Toronto: University of Toronto Press.

James, A., Curtis, P. & Birch, J. (2008) Care and Control in the Construction of Children's Citizenship, in A. Invernizzi & J. Williams (Eds) *Children and Citizenship.* London: SAGE.

James, A., Jencks, C. & Prout, A. (1998) *Theorizing Childhood.* Cambridge: Polity Press.

Kalantzis, M. & Cope, B. (2010) New Media, New Learning, in D.R. Cole & D. Pullen (Eds) *Multiliteracies in Motion: current theory and practice.* New York: Routledge.

Keet, A. & Carrim, N. (2006) Human Rights Education and Curricular Reform in South Africa, *Journal of Social Science Education,* 5, 87-105.

Lansdown, G. (2001) *Promoting Children's Participation in Democratic Decision-making.* Florence, Italy: Innocenti UNICEF.

Lapayese, Y. (2005) National Initiatives in Human Rights Education: the implementation of human rights education policy reform in schools, in J. Zajda (Ed.) *International Handbook on Globalisation, Education and Policy Research.* Dordrecht: Springer. http://dx.doi.org/10.1007/1-4020-2960-8_25

Locke, J. (1690/1959) *An Essay Concerning Human Understanding.* New York: Dover.

Luke, C. (1989) *Pedagogy, Printing and Protestantism.* Albany: State University of New York Press.

Lundy, L., Kilkelly, U., Byrne, B. & Kang, J. (2012) The UN Convention on the Rights of the Child: a study of legal implementation in 12 countries. http://www.unicef.org.uk/Documents/Publications/UNICEFUK_2012CRCim plementationreport FINAL PDF version.pdf

McGowan, T. (2012) Human Rights within Education: assessing the justifications, *Cambridge Journal of Education,* 42, 67-81. http://dx.doi.org/10.1080/0305764X.2011.651204

Millei, Z. & Imre, R. (2009) The Problems with Using the Concept 'Citizenship' in Early Years Policy, *Contemporary Issues in Early Childhood,* 10, 280-290. http://dx.doi.org/10.2304/ciec.2009.10.3.280

Morrow, V. (1994) Responsible Children? Aspects of Children's Work and Employment Outside School in Contemporary UK, in B. Myall (Ed.) *Children's Childhoods Observed and Experienced.* London: Falmer.

National Children's Commissioner (2013) *Children's Rights Report 2013.* Sydney: Australian Human Rights Commission.

National Children's Commissioner (2014) *Children's Rights Report 2014.* Sydney: Australian Human Rights Commission.

Office of the High Commissioner for Human Rights (2015) First Phase (2005-2009) of the World Programme for the Human Rights Education: national action plans/strategies for human rights education. http://www.ohchr.org/EN/Issues/Education/Training/WPHRE/FirstPhase/Pa ges/NationalActionsPlans.aspx

Perry, B. (2013) *Children, Film and Literacy*. Basingstoke: Palgrave Macmillan. http://dx.doi.org/10.1057/9781137294333

Phillips, L.G. (2014) I Want to Do Real Things: explorations of children's active community participation, in J. Davis & S. Elliott (Eds) *Research in Early Childhood Education for Sustainability: international perspectives and provocations*. Abingdon: Routledge.

Phillips, L.G. & Hickey, A. (2013) Child Led Tours of Brisbane's Fortitude Valley as Public Pedagogy, *International Journal of Pedagogies and Learning*, 8, 242-253. http://dx.doi.org/10.5172/ijpl.2013.8.3.242

Piaget, J. (1932) *The Moral Judgment of the Child*. London: Kegan Paul, Trench, Trubner.

Quennerstedt, A. (2011) The Political Construction of Children's Rights in Education: a comparative analysis of Sweden and New Zealand, *Education Inquiry*, 2, 453-471. http://dx.doi.org/10.3402/edui.v2i3.21994

Ramirez, F.O., Suarez, D. & Meyer, J.W. (2006) The Worldwide Rise of Human Rights Education, in A. Benavot & C. Braslavsky (Eds) *School Knowledge in Comparative and Historical Perspective: changing curricula in primary and secondary education*. Hong Kong: Comparative Education Research Centre (CERC) and Springer.

Robinson, C. (2014a) Children, Their Voices and Their Experiences of School: what does the evidence tell us? CPRT Research Survey 2. Cambridge Primary Review Trust.

Robinson, C. (2014b) Developing Mutually Respectful Adult-child Relationships in Schools: is this a reality experienced equally by all pupils? *Research Intelligence*, 18-19.

Rousseau, J. (1762/2007) *Emile: or, on education*. Sioux Falls, SD: Nu Vision.

Saunders, B.J. & Goddard, C. (2002) *The Role of Mass Media in Facilitating Community Education and Child Abuse Prevention Strategies*. Melbourne: Australian Institute of Family Studies.

Schmid, J., Wilson, T. & Taback, R. (2010) Soul Buddyz Clubs: a social development innovation, *International Social Work*, 54, 272-286. http://dx.doi.org/10.1177/0020872810369120

Sebba, J. & Robinson, C. (2010) Evaluation of UNICEF UK's Rights Respecting Schools Award. Universities of Sussex and Brighton.

Soul City Institute (2015) Soul City Institute Health & Development communication. http://www.soulcity.org.za/projects/soul-buddyz (accessed 2 November 2015).

Tibbitts, F. (2002) Understanding What We Do: emerging models for human rights education, *International Review of Education*, 48, 159-171. http://dx.doi.org/10.1023/A:1020338300881

Tibbitts, F. (2009) *Impact Assessment of Rights Education Leading to Action Programme (REAP)*. Norway: Amnesty International.

Tibbitts, F. & Fernekes, W. (2011) Human Rights Education, in S. Totten & J.E. Pedersen (Eds) *Teaching and Studying Social Issues: major programs and approaches*. Charlotte, NC: Information Age.

UN Committee on the Rights of the Child (2001) General Comment No. 1 (2001), Article 29(1), The Aims of Education. http://www.ohchr.org/EN/Issues/Education/Training/Compilation/Pages/a%29GeneralCommentNo1TheAimsofEducation%28article29%29%282001%29.aspx

UN Committee on the Rights of the Child (2012) Consideration of Reports Submitted by States Parties under Article 44 of the Convention: concluding observations: Australia. http://www2.ohchr.org/english/bodies/crc/docs/co/CRC_C_AUS_CO_4.pdf

UNESCO (2006) *Plan of Action: world programme for human rights education – first phase.* New York: UNESCO.

UNICEF (2006) *Assessing Child Friendly Schools: a guide for programme managers in East Asia and the Pacific.* Bangkok: UNICEF East Asia/Pacific Regional Office.

UNICEF (2009) *Manual: Child Friendly Schools.* New York: UNICEF.

UNICEF Canada (2011) *Rights Respecting Schools: a snapshot.* Canada: UNICEF.

UNICEF UK (n.d.) *Rights Respecting Schools Award: a quick guide.* London: UNICEF.

UNICEF/UNESCO (2007) *A Human Rights-based Approach to Education for All,* New York: UNICEF.

United Nations General Assembly (1948) Universal Declaration of Human Rights. http://daccess-dds-ny.un.org/doc/RESOLUTION/GEN/NR0/043/88/IMG/NR004388.pdf?OpenElement

United Nations General Assembly (1989) Convention on the Rights of the Child. New York: United Nations.

Waksler, F.C. (1991) Studying Children: phenomenological insights, in F.C. Waksler (Ed.) *Studying the Social Worlds of Children: sociological readings.* London: Falmer.

World Conference on Human Rights (1993) Vienna Declaration and Programme of Action World Conference A/CONF.157/23. Vienna.

CHAPTER 3

Human Rights Education: teaching children's human rights – a matter of why, what and how

NINA THELANDER

SUMMARY This chapter is about human rights education. It takes off from the United Nations Convention on the Rights of the Child and from the World Plan of Action programmes for human rights education with a specific focus on teaching children's human rights and what that might mean in terms of (a) knowledge and skills, (b) values, attitudes and behaviour, and (c) action to defend and promote human rights. By using examples from a case study in Sweden, a discussion of what teaching children's human rights might be in primary school is initiated together with a general discussion of the questions of what, why and how the content of human rights education are and could be addressed in schools.

Introduction

Human rights education, which has been a subject of interest within the international community for many years, is influenced by processes of globalisation developed over time. Since the Second World War a global society has grown and developed based on ideas of peace building and tolerance among communities, making human rights education an important aspect. This has led to a change from national to global conceptions of human rights, and human rights education has shifted from being a national concern to a global matter. It could also be argued that concepts of global human rights have an increasing impact on national school systems, educational policies and national curricula. Human rights education moreover is put forth as reflecting both an evolving emphasis on world citizenship and the strong assumption of individual agency required for global citizenship (Ramirez et al, 2007).

Human rights education became a particularly crucial issue after the World Conference on Human Rights in Vienna in 1993 (Baxi, 1994, Suárez, 2007). The conference resulted in the Vienna Declaration and Programme for Action (UN General Assembly, 1993), which asserted human rights education as 'essential for the promotion and achievement of stable and harmonious relations among communities and for fostering mutual understanding, tolerance and peace' (UN General Assembly, 1993, p. 18). Two years later, the United Nations (UN) declared the years 1995 to 2014 to be the 'Decade of Human Rights Education', whose aims were further advanced and reformed in the 'Plans of Action for the Decade of Human Rights Education' (UNHCR, 2005). Since the introduction of the UN Decade, human rights education has been elaborated upon in various documents and implemented on national levels, for instance as national plans of action, and in formal school curricula and syllabuses.[1] In addition, numerous initiatives by intergovernmental and non-governmental organisations have been taken, which have resulted in more actions and programmes, all with the aim of assisting the implementation processes of global human rights education, especially in formal education (Volker & Savolainen, 2002). In 2011 a new declaration, the Declaration of Human Rights Education and Training (UNHCR, 2011), was adopted by the General Assembly, which was a clear signal from the international community that human rights education is to be taken seriously.

The Vienna Declaration and its adjoining Plans of Action are examples of the development of global movements for human rights education that are having a growing impact on national policies and curricula around the world. This impact often goes beyond national ideas about education and national citizenship (Ramirez et al, 2007). Originally an issue of several different concerns, mostly focusing on having access to education, human rights education has become a topic of broader perspectives, where discussions and actions underline the aims of the education in a stronger and more detailed way than before. The Plans of Action centre on several target groups. The focus of the first phase is on human rights education in primary and secondary school systems, with a presentation of strategies and practical guidelines for implementing human rights education in primary and secondary schools.

In this chapter the main concern is human rights education for children and young people and it will say something about its *past*, *present* and *future*. A specific focus is its role and aims for educating children and young people *about* and *on* human rights in formal education. Guiding questions are: 'What is human rights education for children and young people in an international perspective and what might human rights education be in a specific school context – in this case, Sweden?' and 'What is teaching human rights and how is it expressed and practised when teachers in Sweden teach human rights in school?'

Human rights education is a central part of the right to education and it shares the same issues of concern as all education. At the same time, it carries specific aims with its own qualities and problems. The intentions and aims of human rights education are formulated in guidelines on both global and national levels, such as the UN Convention on the Rights of the Child (CRC) (United Nations, 1989), the World Programme for Human Rights Education (UNHCR, 2005), the Plans of Action and various national curricula and syllabuses. Instructions concerning the aims of human rights education and ideological ideas and conceptions are built into the different documents. Like all education, human rights education needs to be viewed and understood in the light of specific historical, political, economic and social contexts. This means that what constitutes good human rights education at one time in one situation is not necessarily considered good in another time and situation. *What is good human rights education today and what might good human rights education be in the future?*

Before approaching the issues of human rights education, especially human rights education for children and young people, a brief background based on selected guiding global documents will be presented to provide insight into the aim of human rights education from an international perspective as well as into the fundamental ideological ideas built into the documents. This is followed by examples from national documents guiding primary education in Sweden. Using empirical data from two Swedish schools, some illustrations of the teaching of human rights will be presented and discussed. Moreover, a discussion of what 'good' human rights education might be will be initiated at the end of the chapter.

Human Rights Education

Human rights education is a construction by the international community, built on values established in international human rights documents. It comprises education *as* a human right and education *for* human rights. In the past few decades we have had an increasing development of programmes and models on the international stage aimed at implementing human rights education within diverse national societies. It has been argued that with the introduction of human rights education, national models for education have been challenged and changed into a more conformist global standard model of the school system (see Ramirez et al, 2007). Moreover, Ramirez et al (2007) explain the increasing impact of human rights education, offering an alternative to the values within the national state, as follows: 'The valued world models for education and society celebrate a world of equality and

63

cooperation, not a world of competition and hierarchy. And they celebrate a world in which the human person is increasingly more central than the national citizen' (p. 6).

However, human rights education is closely linked to international human rights documents embracing the right to education. In the following I will look more closely at the human right to education.

The human right to education is stated in various international instruments, the best known of which is the Universal Declaration of Human Rights (UN General Assembly, 1948). It is also stipulated in the International Covenant on Economic, Social and Cultural Rights (UN General Assembly, 1966) and the Convention on the Rights of the Child (UN General Assembly, 1989), where it is more specifically directed towards children. The right to education is also established in more regional human rights documents around the world, such as the African Charter on Human and Peoples' Rights (Organisation of African Unity, 1981) and the European Convention on Human Rights (Council of Europe, 1950). Characteristic of these earlier human rights documents is that the right to education underscores the importance of the parents' right to choose education, which in turn is historically grounded, based on ideas from the certain time and situation when the documents were formulated. In emphasizing the parents' right to choose education for their children it also underlined parental responsibility and served as a means of limiting the control of education by the state and preventing education from being used as an instrument of indoctrination, as was the case, for example, during the Second World War (Hägglund et al, 2013).

Although the right to education is stated in all of the above documents, it is only in the Convention on the Rights of the Child (UN General Assembly, 1989) that it is explicitly directed towards the child and thereby embraces the child as a holder of the right to education. This shift in perspective reflects a specific view of the position of the child and the child's right to education and is found throughout the CRC in its underlying ideas about children and childhood. In the following, the historical background of the CRC will be briefly presented, along with central ideas about children and young people outlined in the convention.

The UN Convention on the Rights of the Child

On 20 November 1989, the General Assembly of the UN adopted the Convention on the Rights of the Child (CRC) in consensus, bringing a long process to an end. Never before had the nations of the international community been so united. The convention was welcomed by many, even if questions were raised about its power and strength. However, by ratifying the convention, the parties of state made a clear symbolic and moral acknowledgement of the child as a full, worthy human being. The convention also stated the importance of the child as a rights-holder with rights of her/his own. Moreover, ratification meant that the state parties agreed to fulfil the intentions of the convention and to regularly report the development and progress of children's situation and welfare to the specific UN committee. This in turn has given the international community a platform that focuses on children's situations and life conditions around the world and discusses them regularly.

Although the CRC marks a new chapter in the history of children's rights, it was not the first international document on the topic. The convention was preceded by three previous declarations of children's rights, all in the wake of two world wars. The first, in 1924, was adopted by the League of Nations and the other two were adopted by the United Nations in 1948 and 1959, respectively. In these early documents the main concerns were on protection and children's right to social welfare – that is, children's needs largely dominated the image. These documents mirrored contemporary society and were particularly directed towards children's vulnerable position in times of war and towards the poor provision of health and social service for children in general (Thelander, 2009). In the process from the first Declaration on Human Rights to the adoption of the CRC many people have been involved in various ways and in different social movements, thus contributing to the process of children's rights (Reynaert et al, 2012).

However, when the CRC came into force, it caused a shift in ideas about the child and childhood. This new image of the child, which was built into the convention, is based on ideas that reflect major concepts of the post–world war society. The new picture of the child shows a universal, competent child with her/his own rights *as well as* a child with a special need for protection and care. The present life of this child is as important as her/his future life as an adult. Moreover, the child of the convention has been given a new position, in the family and in the society, and is viewed as a competent individual with a capacity to act and participate in all matters that affect her/him.

During the same period of time, along with the working process of the CRC and harmonising with the new ideas about the child and childhood, there was growing interest in the field of the sociology of childhood. Common discussions and studies within this research area have dealt with the child as an active agent and with the child as both dependent and independent, along with discussions about childhood and/or childhoods (see James et al, 1998, James & James, 2004). This growing interest in the individual child, as was the focus in the CRC, rather than on children in general, coincides with and is in line with today's individualised society, which also embraces the importance of the individual as a competent active agent (for further reading, see Beck, 2007; Ramirez et al, 2007). In this way it can be said that the CRC is a document of its time.

As much as the adoption of the CRC represents the end of a long process it was also the starting point for the process of implementation of human rights for children and young people around the world, which continues to this day. The CRC consists of more than 50 articles encompassing all categories of civil, political, social, economic and cultural rights. A common way of approaching the content of the CRC is to use the guiding principles from four of the articles: the right to non-discrimination (Article 2); the best interest of the child (Article 3); the right to development (Article 6); and the right to be heard and listened to (Article 12). These articles are not intended to be viewed as more important than others, but they often have a specific position in interpretations of the convention, indicating that they are more of a focus of attention than the others.

In the implementation work concerning children's rights, pre-schools and schools are important institutions and much effort has been spent in fulfilling the intentions of children's and young people's right to education. Nonetheless, many children and young people around the world cannot make use of their right to education.

Generally, when reading of the articles of the CRC, the right to education is viewed as a dual concept – that is, the right *to* education and the right *in* and *through* education. The right to education is divided into two articles, Article 28 and Article 29. Article 28 lays down the right *to* education, including access to education; Article 29 is directed towards the aim of education. With this broader definition of the right to education it is clear that having access to education is not enough. Everyday experience, together with the content of learning in education, is also of utmost importance.

Definitions of the right to education have been the focus of previous research; for example, McCowan (2010) makes an important distinction between education and schooling, claiming that the right to education has often been discussed as the same as the right to schooling. He clarifies the distinction by showing that school can be a place without education, while education can take place without going to school. At the same time, he also demonstrates that education and school often go hand in hand. His main criticism is directed towards the formulations and definitions of human rights documents when it comes to the right to education. In his argumentation he underlines the importance of viewing the right to education from a broader perspective and together with aspects of quality, arguing that the right to education is also about what pupils learn and what they gain in the form of experience through participation in educational activities. This is not sufficiently clear, McCowan (2010) maintains, in the human rights documents. At the same time, the CRC has a broader perspective of the right to education in Article 29, outlining the aim of education:

1. State Parties agree that the education of the child shall be directed to:
(a) The development of the child's personality, talents and mental and physical abilities to their fullest potential;
(b) The development of respect for human rights and fundamental freedoms, and for the principles enshrined in the Charter of the United Nations;
(c) The development of respect for the child's parents, his or her own cultural identity, language and values, for the national values of the country in which the child is living, the country from which he or she may originate, and for civilizations different from his or her own;
(d) The preparation of the child for responsible life in a free society, in the spirit of understanding, peace, tolerance, equality of sexes, and friendship among all peoples, ethnic, national and religious groups and persons of indigenous origin;
(e) The development of respect for the natural environment.

Article 29 outlines the aim of education, particularly stressing the importance of fostering democratic citizens and teaching them peace, tolerance and equality. Moreover, another central concern is to develop respect for human rights and to respect the child's parents, cultural identity, language and values. Article 29 has also been discussed by the UN Committee on the Rights of the Child and clarified in one of the committee's General Comments, discussing the aim of education and highlighting its need to be child-centred, child-friendly and empowering (UN Committee on the Rights of the Child, 2001).

In school, where the right to education is practised, the general assignment is often described in terms of knowledge and values education. In this context it is interesting to note that not much is said in the CRC about knowledge related to school subjects or skills. Even though it is possible to interpret knowledge in the writings of Article 29, it is not explicitly formulated as a right in the convention. On the other hand, issues related to values are outlined and emphasised all the more in the article, as in the General Comments of the UN Committee (UN Committee on the Rights of the Child, 2001). This indicates that values education is a matter of higher interest to the convention and the committee, and issues relating to children's right to specific knowledge is a question that should be discussed and organised in national discussions (Hägglund et al, 2013). The fact that issues related to knowledge seem to be more of a national issue than outlined in the aim of human rights education was pointed out in a study by Quennerstedt (2011). Analysing children's rights policies in two countries, Sweden and New Zealand, her comparison showed that pupils' knowledge and level of knowledge are considered a question of pupils' rights on a national level but that this is not emphasised specifically in the CRC. This shows that there are variations in global and national conceptions of human rights, especially as related to knowledge. At the same time it illustrates the need for a contextualisation of human rights education.

This has been a discussion of the historical background of the CRC and the ideas about children that are built into the discourse on children's rights, including the right to education and the aim of education, which were broadened through the establishment of the convention. In the following, the Plans of Action for the World Programme for Human Rights Education will be the focus.

Plans of Action: World Programme for Human Rights Education

The UN Decade for Human Rights Education can be described as the starting point for various activities and programmes around the world. In 2004, when the decade was over, the General Assembly adopted the World Programme for Human Rights Education (2005-ongoing) (UNHCR, 2005) on 10 December, Human Rights Day, to improve the overall implementation of human rights education. The world programme is divided into three phases, all called a Plan of Action, each plan being directed to a specific target group. The first phase, or the Plan of Action for 2005-2009, which is the focus of this article, involved primary and secondary school systems. The second phase, 2010-2014, was aimed at human rights education in higher education and human rights training for civil servants, law enforcement officers and the military. It was also intended to strengthen the implementation of the first phase. The Plan of Action for the third phase (2015-2019) is set to strengthen the first two phases and to support human rights training for media professionals and journalists.

In the Plan of Action for 2005-2009 specific guidelines for six different areas were formulated, including human rights education in the school system, which correlates with the General Comments of the UN Committee regarding the aim of education (UN Committee on the Rights of the Child, 2001). Human rights education was also described as a way of improving the effectiveness of national school systems by promoting child-friendly learning environments and the like. There were also strategies for implementation at the national level, including international cooperation and support. Moreover, human rights education was defined as threefold: *education*, *training* and *information*, all aimed at building up a universal culture of human rights. As a whole, the Plan of Action stretched over a range of areas and defined some of the particular aspects.

Three aspects that were specifically outlined as a definition of human rights education were:

1. Knowledge and skills;
2. Values, attitudes and behaviour;
3. Action.

The first aspect identified human rights as a knowledge area with a specific content of learning and recognised certain important skills that needed to be developed in order to practise the content learnt as well as to protect human rights. The second aspect emphasised the importance of strengthening and advancing values and attitudes that uphold human rights. The third aspect not only dealt with protecting and promoting human rights but also emphasised the importance of taking action to defend them.

In the Plan of Action for 2005-2009 components of human rights education were presented which were described as based on studies, research and successful experiences around the world. Further information or explicit references to research and experience were not provided. According to the Plan, the components were meant to be indicative, not prescriptive. One of the components was teaching and learning, within which there were guidelines to help fulfil the requirements of a holistic approach to teaching and learning. In these guidelines, proposals were addressed to both policy-makers and teachers, urging them to adopt experience-based learning methods that would enable pupils to learn by doing, putting human rights into practice (UNHCR, 2005, p. 46).

As pointed out above, the Plan of Action was part of the discourse of the global society. In the following we will use the three aspects that define human rights education – *knowledge and skills*, *values, attitudes and behaviour*, and *actions* – as tools for analysing planned teaching activities in a national context. This will be done through two examples from Sweden.

Teaching Children's Human Rights: the Swedish context

While the focus so far has been on human rights education on an international level, here the focus will be on actions in the school and particularly on teaching human rights on the national level – namely, in Sweden. In Sweden, as in many other western countries, demands to improve pupils' achievements have been raised in national political and general public debates of the past few decades. These debates often refer to international measurements like the Programme for International Student Assessment (PISA) and the Trends in International Mathematics and Science Study (TIMMS) and to pupils' declining knowledge, followed by demands for change and better results from the educational sector. Moreover, the test results have been used not only in discussions of education, but also as vital aspects and tools on the international arena when discussing economic strength on the global market. Through the decentralisation of the school system in Sweden, followed by parental choice and school competition, the Swedish school system can be described as market-orientated, like many other nations in Western Europe. This has been followed in many countries by a strong emphasis on documenting pupils' knowledge and development and on evaluating and assessing the schools (for further reading, see e.g. Apple, 2006).

In this connection, reformation of the policy documents for Swedish primary schools was carried out, for example in the Education Act of 2010 and the 2011 curriculum (Swedish Ministry of Education and Science, 2011). This reformation called for higher and more detailed knowledge requirements in each subject and for a new grading system. At the same time, another system of assessment was reintroduced in Swedish middle schools, including both formative and summative assessments. Summative assessments had not been used in middle schools for more than 30 years, so this form of assessment tool created some worries and uncertainties among teachers and pupils in the implementation phase. Now, the subject matter, the knowledge content and the new knowledge requirement are given much more weight in teaching and learning in Swedish middle schools.

Another adjustment of special interest here is that knowledge of human rights and especially of the CRC is given further stress in the policy documents. At the core of the curriculum special emphasis was given to the content of human rights and their meaning and importance, including the rights of the child under the CRC (Swedish Ministry of Education and Science, 2011, p. 19). At the same time as human rights are given more emphasis in the policy documents it would appear that children's human rights are considered to be separate and not a part of human rights (Hägglund et al, 2013).

Human rights and children's human rights are stressed in the curriculum but foremost in the syllabus for civics. In the curriculum for primary school human rights are expressed within *norms and values* and as a *specific knowledge content*. In the aim for the subject of civics, it is outlined that teaching will help pupils develop a familiarity with human rights, and through teaching, pupils will be given opportunities to develop their ability and skills to reflect on human rights. Moreover, human rights are underlined as a central content within the syllabus for civics for years 4-6. In the knowledge requirements within the syllabus, the aim is to describe the meaning of human rights and children's human rights and to be able to exemplify the meaning of rights in other parts of the world. The stronger emphasis here on human rights as a specific knowledge content is in line with the items for human rights education as outlined in the Plan of Action.

Taken together, the process of implementing the reformed policy documents has drawn attention, from different directions, to issues related to teaching in general, especially teaching specific subjects, as well as issues related to higher knowledge requirements and/or their connection to assessments and grading. This has opened the area up for questions concerning *what* and *how* teachers teach children and young people children's rights in school. The empirical material presented here is drawn from a main study about teaching civics in the Swedish middle school.

The examples here have been taken from two teachers, Sven and Karl (these are pseudonyms), and their planned activities surrounding children's human rights in two middle schools in Sweden. The interests here is when the teachers talk about their experiences and discuss the content and design of their planned activities. The examples are from interviews conducted during planning, implementation and the final phases.

As a tool for analysing the data, the three aspects above defining human rights education – *knowledge and skills, values, attitudes and behaviour*, and *action* – will be used. The guiding questions in this section are: What is human rights education in a Swedish school context? and What human rights are expressed and practised in teaching them, and how?

Middle schools in Sweden encompass years 4-6 of primary school. In many schools one teacher is responsible for teaching almost all the subjects in one class for all three years. The teachers in this study are such teachers, responsible for all the activities of the 16 subjects taught at the school.

Sven and Karl each have more than 10 years of experience as teachers. In Sven's class, which at the time was year 5, there were 22 pupils. In Karl's class, year 6, there were 13 pupils. Sven's school was in a town and Karl's school was in the countryside just outside the town, but they worked together. When discussing their activities about children's rights they planned for 10-12 lessons. They also carried out their planning and discussions with other teachers in the group.

Children's Human Rights: what and how?

Sven and Karl began to plan their activities by formulating a pedagogical plan showing *why, what* and *how* they were going to work with the topic of children's rights. The plan was directed to both teachers and pupils. Through an assessment matrix the pupils could find the requirements for achieving certain grades.

In their planned activities Sven and Karl focused on four different topics, which constituted the projects the pupils were to work with in small groups. The projects were about *children's rights in school, children's rights within the family, children's rights in different ages* and *children's rights to children's basic needs.*

The teachers organised their pupils into four groups, one group for each theme. During the lessons the pupils stayed in their project groups and prepared their presentations on their theme. When the projects were finished they presented them in various ways, as theatre, short films or PowerPoints, to their classmates and teachers in the class.

Because there is little material in the schools about children's rights, Karl and Sven constructed a booklet about them to be used as basic educational material. It was based on texts from various websites, mostly non-governmental organisations such as Save the Children, and from a website published by the government. In an effort to transform the material and make things clearer for the pupils, they 'cut and pasted and made a dictionary of difficult words' (Sven). In this booklet, which was handed out to all the pupils, the pupils could find texts like the Convention on the Rights of Children in a short version. In addition, each group received a booklet on their own specific project. The projects were divided into the themes found in the human rights material from the government website on human rights. According to Karl and Sven, children's rights are abstract and hard for the pupils to grasp and therefore they felt a need to transform the accessible material into a booklet that would simplify and concretise the material for the pupils.

In the following, examples will be presented that illustrate different aspects of human rights education as they appeared in the data. The guiding questions for each aspect were once again *what* and *how*, starting with the aspect of *knowledge and skills*.

Knowledge and Skills

It isn't always easy to grasp the content of the CRC, not even for teachers. In Sven and Karl's discussions about what content they wanted to use, Karl found himself exclaiming, 'What is knowledge in the convention [really], is it just being able to rattle article after article or what *feeling* do we have for the convention?'

The most important piece of content knowledge about human rights, according to Karl and Sven, is to be familiar with and have an awareness of the CRC. This is done by reading the articles in the convention, especially the guiding principles, in class and as homework. At home the pupils were encouraged to discuss the CRC with their parents and the following day discuss it in class, in order to understand the abstract articles. After this, pupils began their project work. An important piece of knowledge, according to Sven, was 'to know why there is a convention and how it might be used in most parts of the world, and in Sweden, and that kind of thing'.

Underlying reasons for the convention and its historical background are also important for the pupils to know, according to Karl and Sven. Another piece of content knowledge they mentioned was being aware of children's vulnerable situations in different times and circumstances, along with an awareness of different children's living conditions throughout the world. Sven went on to say, 'They need to have a sense of the intentions of the convention, as this is a kind of "security guarantee" in an unsafe world. It's important for the pupils to have knowledge of this.'

The teachers felt it was important that the pupils knew the articles in the convention and its background and were able to show an awareness of the vulnerable position of children in various situations in society. Questions like 'What is the convention and why do we have it?', 'Is it really necessary?' and 'Would we be okay without it?' were all mentioned by the teachers as issues they wished to raise with the pupils.

In addition, Karl also highlighted the importance of having deeper knowledge about the articles in the convention when he talked about the need for the pupils 'to be able to practise and relate their work in the project to the convention'.

By using different themes, the pupils probably obtained a more varied and holistic view of the convention. Sven described examples of pupil presentations related to daily situations at home, with parents and children; situations in school, with harassment and bullying; and the situation for children in a country involved in war.

Being able to apply the articles to situations in their projects and everyday life is a skill the teachers would like the pupils to practise and learn from. Another important skill that was highlighted in the interviews was being able to make a good presentation, in particular communicating it well.

Within the aspect of *knowledge and skills*, the specific content of what should be learnt was basically the same as the CRC and its articles. At the same time as it can be said that the teachers had a rather narrow perspective of children's human rights, it is probably also a common way of organising teaching about children's rights in Swedish schools. I would argue that the examples show a broader perspective when historical situations were used to explain today's situation in both Sweden and other countries. Discussions of different children's living conditions, for example, made this possible. It was not only the teachers who taught – the pupils themselves, guided by the teachers, developed skills in how to apply articles of human rights to specific situations.

Values, Attitudes and Behaviour

This aspect emphasises the importance of strengthening and advancing values, attitudes and behaviours that uphold human rights.

In the interviews the teachers expressed a stronger emphasis on this aspect than the others. It was highlighted and valued more in the earlier policy documents as well. With increased knowledge requirements and focus on knowledge content, the teachers found it harder to encourage pupils to be engaged and active in discussions, even though this was not explicitly expressed in the knowledge requirements for this topic. This might be explained by the fact that the study was conducted during the period when the policy documents were being implemented.

However, when the pupils worked in groups, the teachers walked around and discussed the projects and gave them a helping hand when needed. Sven described the discussions thus: 'We do have a dialogue, we listen to each other, and I think this is the key, in some way, to having a dialogue with the pupils.' Having an encouraging attitude towards the pupils' ideas regarding how they wanted to present their work, for instance, was viewed as significant for the pupils' growth. Working in groups is not always an easy task, the teachers admitted, but it is a good way for pupils to practise values and principles that characterise a democratic society. Making a presentation, for example, requires teamwork and arranging a number of different things. How to divide up the work within the group was sometimes a subject of discussion.

Both Sven and Karl talked a great deal about encouraging pupils to express their opinions, to be independent human beings. Karl, for instance, said, 'I want them to think by themselves, be independent human beings, not just swallow [any old thing]; you know, if you think, [if you] come up with ideas and give suggestions, then everything is so much easier.'

In line with the content of children's human rights, the teachers strove to support values and attitudes like tolerance and the right to be listened to and other democratic values. A friendly and encouraging dialogue seemed to be a strong ingredient in this work.

Actions

The third aspect had to do with actions to protect, promote and defend human rights. Karl and Sven both spoke of the importance for the pupils to be able to take action, especially when related to children in vulnerable situations. They underlined the significance of the individual child knowing and being aware of difficult situations where the CRC could be a practical tool for action. Moreover, the importance of having caring peers and adults around them who were aware of children's rights, as well as helping them to become protectors of other children's rights, was also emphasised.

Taking action can also have to do with being able to express your opinion and be listened to in school. This action is practised within this aspect and is also something the teachers actively tried to let the pupils do in their everyday practice. It was also expressed, to some extent, by the teachers when discussing children's rights. From what is found in the interviews, this seems to be more a question of training for future situations and a way of preparing pupils to take action when situations arise.

What is more is that the aspects outlined as defining human rights education are closely intertwined, with some situations containing qualities of all them, which sometimes made it difficult to separate them from each other. Nonetheless, it is clear that they can be used to capture *what* children's human rights education is practised, and *how*.

In previous research on schoolchildren's views of schoolchildren's rights in Kenya and Sweden, pupils shared a view of the CRC as first and foremost a problem-solver, especially for vulnerable children in need. The convention was regarded 'as a tool for emergencies', while its relevance seemed rather unclear and vague for ordinary children and their life conditions. The convention was talked about and described by both Kenyan and Swedish pupils as necessary – however, more so by children in Africa, whom both groups referred to as being more vulnerable and exposed (Thelander, 2009).

Just as the schoolchildren in Kenya and Sweden talked about the CRC as a problem-solver, so did the teachers. This view can also be found in the four themes, as described above, that guided the pupils' project work regarding children's rights in various situations.

Based on the interviews, Sven and Karl seemed to strive towards making their teaching both child-friendly and empowering for their pupils. If the CRC is the main answer to the question of *what* teachers teach within human rights education, the answer to the question of *how* the teaching is expressed is more diverse. Teaching human rights seems to be open to other ways of working with subjects than the traditional ones.

In this section I used the different aspects that define human rights education as laid out in the Plan of Action as analytical tools to explore human rights education in a specific school context. My intent was to answer the question outlined in this section: *what* human rights are expressed and practised in a Swedish school context, and *how* are they taught?

The main knowledge content in these examples is found in the CRC, which also correlates with specific knowledge requirements outlined in the Swedish curriculum (Swedish Ministry of Education and Science, 2011).

As the empirical material here was mainly based on interviews with two teachers, it should be viewed as providing *examples* of human rights education in Sweden, which in turn were grounded in established ideas about education and human rights in a Swedish context.

Concluding Remarks

The main concern of this chapter has been human rights education for children and young people. By way of introduction it was stated that the aim of human rights education, like all education, is based on specific ideological ideas and needs to be understood in the light of historical, political, economic and social contexts. In brief, human rights education, including international human rights documents, can be viewed as responses to, and built upon, ideas that developed in the wake of two world wars. Bearing in mind that fundamental ideas like 'all people are born equal' have a much longer historical background, it is in post-war modern society that international documents were first formulated, usually within the international community as represented by the United Nations.

The human rights education documents prescribe a specific model of education and school system, which is both valued and criticised. When valued, it is celebrated as a challenge to market-orientated models and as an alternative to the national citizen. The global model also embraces equality and cooperation and places the human being before the national citizen. Moreover, it holds a critique of national market-orientated school systems that prescribe competition and parental choice (see Apple, 2006; Ramirez et al, 2007).

When criticised, it is mainly for exporting a conformist model of education systems that embraces western values, which does not always appeal to other social and economic systems. And what does it mean when the Plan of Action for 2005-2009 emphasised that human rights education is an important tool for improving the effectiveness of national education systems?

In the policy documents for human rights education emerging from the international community, the focus has been on fundamental democratic values and various categories of rights. The aim of human rights education is to build a universal culture of human rights, through educational training and information. In the Swedish context, based on the two examples, human rights education seems to be limited to children's human rights; general human rights are not brought up when talking about and to children. At the same time, it is apparent that children's human rights have become a matter of content knowledge in the Swedish primary school.

As demonstrated, what characterises good human rights education can be found in two parallel paths, the global society and various national contexts. From a Swedish perspective, they can be viewed as complementing each other.

In the above I have tried to outline what good human rights education might be today and tried to show that ideas embedded in actions and tragedies from the past influence society of today.

At the time of writing, the largest refugee tragedy of our time is taking place within Europe, a situation so complex that it is impossible to grasp. At the same time as politicians and public debaters discuss how to solve the situation in Europe on the regional and national level, antidemocratic and xenophobic movements are on the rise, both inside and outside national borders. Another concern of the political and public debates in Europe is the issue of democracy. Taken together, we see a blurry picture of a future political and social situation that may well challenge our values and ideas. Hopefully, our experiences from the past and today's global and national human rights education will be important building blocks for human rights education in the future.

Note

[1] Not all countries have a national action plan. Examples of those who do are Australia, France, Germany, Sweden, Ethiopia, Tanzania and Peru (see UN Human Rights Office of the High Commissioner, 2005).

References

Apple, M.W. (2006) Producing Inequalities: neo-liberalism, neo-conservatism and the politics of educational reform, in H. Lauder, P. Brown, J. Dillabough & A.H. Halsey (Eds) *Education, Globalization and Social Change*, pp. 468-489. Oxford: Oxford University Press.

Baxi, U. (1994) Human Rights Education: the promise of the third millennium? http://eric.ed.gov/?id=ED409221 (accessed 23 September 2015).

Beck, U. (2007) Beyond Class and Nation: reframing social inequalities in a globalizing world, *British Journal of Sociology*, 58(4), 679-705. http://dx.doi.org/10.1111/j.1468-4446.2007.00171.x

Council of Europe (1950) Convention for the Protection of Human Rights and Fundamental Freedoms (European Convention on Human Rights, as Amended) (ECHR) Art 3, 1950.

Hägglund, S., Quennerstedt, A. & Thelander, N. (2013) *Barns och ungas rättigheter i utbildning*, 1st edn. Malmö: Gleerups Utbildning.

James, A. & James, A.L. (2004) *Constructing Childhood: theory, policy, and social practice*. New York: Palgrave Macmillan.

James, A., Jenks, C. & Prout, A. (1998) *Theorizing Childhood*. Cambridge: Polity Press.

McCowan, T. (2010) Reframing the Universal Right to Education, *Comparative Education*, 46(4), 509-525. http://dx.doi.org/10.1080/03050068.2010.519482

Organisation of African Unity (1981) African Charter on Human and Peoples' Rights OAU Doc. CAB/LEG/67/3 rev. 5, 21 I.L.M. 58 (1982), entered into force 21 October 1986.

Quennerstedt, A. (2011) The Political Construction of Children's Rights in Education: a comparative analysis of Sweden and New Zealand, *Education Inquiry*, 2(3), 453-471. http://dx.doi.org/10.3402/edui.v2i3.21994

Ramirez, F.O., Suárez, D. & Meyer, J.W. (2007) The Worldwide Rise of Human Rights Education, in A. Benavot & C. Braslavsky (Eds) *School Knowledge in Comparative and Historical Perspective*, pp. 35-52. Dordrecht: Springer.

Reynaert, D., Bouverne-De Bie, M. & Vandevelde, S. (2012) Between 'Believers' and 'Opponents': critical discussions on children's rights, *International Journal of Children's Rights*, 20(1), 155-168. http://dx.doi.org/10.1163/157181812X626417

Suárez, D. (2007) Education Professionals and the Construction of Human Rights Education, *Comparative Education Review*, 51(1), 48-70. http://dx.doi.org/10.1086/508638

Swedish Ministry of Education and Science (2011) Curriculum for Compulsory Schools (Lgr 11). Stockholm: Ministry of Education and Science in Sweden.

Thelander, N. (2009) We Are All the Same, But...: Kenyan and Swedish school children's views on children's rights. Dissertation, Karlstad University.

United Nations (1998) *The United Nations Decade for Human Rights Education, 1995-2004*. New York: United Nations.

United Nations Committee on the Rights of the Child (2001) CRC General Comment No. 1: the aims of education, 17 April 2001, CRC/GC/2001/1. http://www.unhcr.org/refworld/docid/4538834d2.html (accessed 23 September 2015).

United Nations General Assembly (1948) Universal Declaration of Human Rights, G.A. res.217A (III).

United Nations General Assembly (1966) International Covenant on Economic, Social and Cultural Rights, G.A. res. 2200A (XXI), 993 UNTS 302, entered into force 3 January 1976.

United Nations General Assembly (1989) Convention on the Rights of the Child, G.A. res. 44/25, 1577 UNTS 3.

United Nations General Assembly (1993) Vienna Declaration and Programme of Action (A/CONF.157/23, 12 July 1993). http://www.refworld.org/docid/3ae6b39ec.html (accessed 21 December 2015).

United Nations Human Rights Office of the High Commissioner (UNHCR) (2005) World Programme for Human Rights Education (2005-ongoing). http://www.ohchr.org/EN/Issues/Education/Training/Pages/Programme.aspx (accessed 21 December 2015).

United Nations Human Rights Office of the High Commissioner (UNHCR) (2011) United Nations Declaration on Human Rights Education and Training (G.A. res. 66/137, 19 December 2011). http://daccess-dds-ny.un.org/doc/UNDOC/GEN/N11/467/04/PDF/N1146704.pdf?OpenElement (accessed 21 December 2015).

Volker, L. & Savolainen, K. (2002) Editorial Introduction: human rights education as a field of practice and of theoretical reflection, *International Review of Education* 48(3/4), 145-158. http://dx.doi.org/10.1023/A:1020382115902

CHAPTER 4

Pupils' Participation in the Finnish Classroom: turning the UN Convention on the Rights of the Child into pedagogical practices

REETTA NIEMI, KRISTIINA KUMPULAINEN & LASSE LIPPONEN

SUMMARY In Finland, the recognition of children's rights to agency and voice in the educational process has a long-standing tradition. These rights are further underscored in the process of developing the new national core curriculum for Finnish preschool and basic education. In addition to emphasising the importance of pupils' voice and agency, the national core curriculum emphasises the social nature of teaching and learning. It also stresses engaging pupils in the process of evaluating and developing the pedagogical practices of the classroom. In this chapter, the authors describe how children's rights to agency and voice have been enacted in the lived pedagogical practices of Finnish primary school education over recent years. They draw on empirical data based on an action research initiative collected in one primary classroom community. They conclude by considering how our learning from the past can guide the future in promoting children's voice and agency in education.

Pupils' voices and participation have received increased attention in the past decade, a development which is often attributed to the ratification of the United Nations Convention on the Rights of the Child (UNCRC, 1989; Lundy, 2007). In Article 12 of the UNCRC, it is stated that a child shall, in particular, be provided with the opportunity to be heard in any judicial and administrative proceedings affecting the child, either directly or through a representative or an appropriate body, in a manner consistent with the procedural rules of national law. Hence, there is growing research interest in listening to pupils' voices and supporting their participation in their school lives (e.g. Fielding, 2007; Frost, 2007; Tangen, 2009; Carrington et al, 2010; Messiou, 2011).

In Finland, the recognition of children's rights to participation in the educational process has been institutionalised. For example, in the Basic Education Act 47 a § 1 mom. (1267/2013) (1998), it is stated that children have a right to participate in the process of planning the curriculum. These rights are further underscored in the new national core curriculum for Finnish preschool and basic education (FNBE, 2014), which will formally come into effect in the year 2016. In addition to emphasising the importance of acknowledging pupils' voices and participation in school communities, the national core curriculum emphasises the social nature of teaching and learning. For example, it focuses on developing pupils' investigative, reflective and communicative competencies across the curriculum. Moreover, it stresses pupils' active participation in the process of evaluating and developing the pedagogical practices of the classroom.

It is common for children's options for participating, expressing their voices and taking part in decision making in the classroom to be organised around specific projects, which are, in many cases, 'add-on' practices in classroom life (Malone & Hartung, 2010, p. 32). For example, children may plan a Christmas event or a special school day. In the approach described here, however, pupils' participation is viewed as a legitimate practice and an organic part of classroom life.

We draw on empirical data based on an action research initiative collected in one primary classroom community in Helsinki between August 2009 and May 2015. The action research study was situated in a suburban primary school district in the city of Helsinki, Finland. One classroom and one teacher joined the study. The number of pupils varied from twenty-three to twenty-six. At the end of the study, there were twenty-four pupils (thirteen girls and eleven boys). The classroom was culturally diverse, and there were several multicultural pupils, two of whom did not speak Finnish as a first language. During the research period, the pupils were aged seven years old to thirteen years old. The teacher in this study is also the researcher and the first author of this chapter.

Parts of this action research have already been reported elsewhere, focusing on the pupils' experiences in classroom practices, the workability of the research method in listening to children's voices, and the workability of the method in improving teacher's practical theory and pedagogical actions (Niemi, Kumpulainen & Lipponen, 2015a,b; Niemi, Kumpulainen, Lipponen & Hilppö, 2015). In this chapter we focus on a dialogue between theory and practice and demonstrate how the new goals set forth by the Finnish National Board of Education (FNBE) in the national core curriculum for pupils' participation in classrooms have already been realised as lived practices in the past, as well as how these practices could be expanded into lived practices in other contexts in the future.

The chapter begins by introducing the concept of participation by drawing on Roger A. Hart's (1992), Harry Shier's (2001), and Laura Lundy's (2007) models of participation. Next we discuss how the goals of promoting pupils' participation and voices are stated in the new national core curriculum (FNBE, 2014) and give examples of how these goals are turned into lived pedagogical practices in a Finnish classroom. In our examples we show how pupils' participation can take place through listening to children's voices and giving them possibilities to communicate and evaluate their learning through different kinds of narratives. At the end of this chapter, we discuss ethical questions related to this study. We also discuss how this study benefits the educational community in other contexts in the future. We conclude this chapter by considering the wider implications of this study concerning classroom practice in Finland and beyond with regard to efforts in acknowledging pupils as active participants and agents in the educational process.

Three Models of Participation

Children's participation has been one of the most debated and examined aspects of the Convention on the Rights of the Child (Lundy, 2007; Lansdown, 2010). One of the reasons for the debates relates to the concept's lack of clarity. For example, it is unclear what is meant by 'participation' in the context of children's rights (Lansdown, 2010).

In the educational literature the concept of participation does not have one shared definition. The concept refers generally to the process of sharing decisions that affect children's lives and the life of the community in which they live. It should start with children and young people themselves – on their own terms, with their visions, dreams, hopes and concerns (Hart, 1992; Shier, 2001; Gresalfi et al, 2009).

According to Thomas (2007, pp. 206-207), participation means affecting the social relations of the communities and/or affecting the political relations of the communities. It is also seen as a fundamental right of citizenship (Hart, 1992). As Hart (1992) puts it, 'It is the means by which a democracy is built and it is a standard against which democracies should be measured.'

In educational literature there are different kinds of models through which pupils' participation can be understood and promoted. One of the most influential models has been Roger A. Hart's (1992) ladder of participation, in which he presents an eight-step model that begins with non-participation: (1) manipulation; (2) decoration; and (3) tokenism. The model ends with degrees of participation: (4) assigned but informed;

(5) consulted and informed; (6) adult initiated, shared decisions with children; (7) child initiated and directed; and (8) child initiated, shared decisions with adults.

Based on Hart's ideas, Harry Shier (2001) developed a model of five levels of participation in addition to supportive questions for the educator:

1. Children are listened to.
2. Children are supported in expressing their views.
3. Children's views are taken into account.
4. Children are involved in the decision-making process.
5. Children share power and responsibility for decision making.

In her work, Laura Lundy (2007) has argued that the successful implementation of Article 12 requires consideration of the implications of four separate factors: space, voice, audience and influence. This model provides a way of conceptualising Article 12 of the UNCRC, which is intended to make decision makers focus on four elements of the provision:

1. Space: children must be given the opportunity to express a view.
2. Voice: children must be facilitated to express their views.
3. Audience: the views must be listened to.
4. Influence: the views must be acted upon as appropriate.

Lundy's model reflects the fact that these elements are interrelated. The first stage ensures the child's right to express a view. The next step is the child's right to have the view given due weight. Because decision-making processes are rarely static, the model acknowledges that, once the child is informed of the extent of his/her influence, the process may begin again (Lundy, 2007).

Next we discuss how these three models of participation are reflected in the Finnish national core curriculum (FNBE, 2014) and the everyday practices of a Finnish primary classroom community.

The Finnish National Core Curriculum and Pupils' Participation

National and local needs also influence the interpretation of 'participation'. For example, in Finland, the definition of 'participation' as a civic right has been connected to the following aspects: having responsibility for the working order of the community; having commitment for improving lives in communities; giving possibilities to speak out and act; and sharing power in a community. In Finland, it is also stated that participation means not only being part of a community, but also having a right to identity in a community, and feeling dignity in a community. In Finland, the concept of participation is also connected to the question of preventing children's marginalisation in communities (Kiilakoski et al, 2012, pp. 14-18).

These goals can be seen in the Finnish national core curriculum for preschool and basic education (FNBE, 2014), which states that each child is unique and needs to be appreciated as she/he is. Each child has a right to become a full member of the society. A child needs encouragement and support, but additionally a child needs to be heard and appreciated. Also, a child's welfare must be taken into account. Lastly, it is also important that a child be capable of building practices and welfare in the community (FNBE, 2014, p. 22).

In the Finnish national core curriculum (FNBE, 2014), children's participation is also related to human rights, democracy and active citizenship. Schools should provide children with communities in which they can build and implement these skills together with others (FNBE, 2014, p. 34). In addition to emphasising the importance of pupils' voices as a form of participation, the national core curriculum emphasises the social nature of teaching and learning. It focuses on developing pupils' skills for active, investigative, reflective and communicative learning. The core curriculum also states that play, the use of imagination and the use of artistic elements in teaching and learning improve pupils' conceptual and methodological knowledge and skills for critical and creative thinking (FNBE, 2014, p. 29). The curriculum stresses engaging pupils in the process of evaluating and developing the pedagogical practices of the classroom. It says that pupils should participate in the process of planning, implementing and evaluating their learning. They should also participate in the process of planning, implementing and evaluating the processes of the school community (FNBE, 2014, p. 23).

The perspectives of participation according to the FNBE (2014) can be summarised in three categories: (1) children's participation in school communities; (2) the social nature of teaching and learning; and (3) children's role in evaluation and school assessment. In the following paragraphs we give examples of how these aspects of participation set forth by the Finnish national core curriculum have been implemented into pedagogical practices in a Finnish classroom.

We start by discussing how pupils' participation was enacted in pedagogical practices through the diamond-ranking method and building wing meetings in a Finnish primary school classroom community. Next we describe how the teacher used narrative learning projects in order to support pupils' participation in teaching and learning. Projects utilised investigative learning in order to study concepts of the phenomena, and various narratives presented learning outcomes that gave pupils an opportunity to express their learning in multiple ways. These are issues that are considered important in teaching and learning in order to improve pupils' conceptual and methodological knowledge and skills for critical and creative thinking (FNBE, 2014, p. 29). We also describe how pupils engaged in the process of creating assessment criteria in these projects.

Supporting Pupils' Participation in the Classroom through a Diamond-ranking Activity

Many researchers have identified photographs as particularly helpful for pupils to document and communicate their perspectives of what constitutes meaningful classroom experiences (Caine, 2010; Niemi, Kumpulainen & Lipponen, 2015a,b; Niemi, Kumpulainen, Lipponen & Hilppö, 2015). During the action research initiative, the method of using photos as a tool to engage pupils with developing classroom practices developed continually during three action research cycles (Niemi, Kumpulainen, Lipponen, 2015a,b; Niemi, Kumpulainen, Lipponen & Hilppö, 2015). The diamond-ranking method, described in this chapter, took place between August 2013 and December 2013.

From the very beginning of the school year, the teacher had two cameras in the classroom. The teacher assigned each camera to a pupil for one week. Pupils who had cameras were then allowed to take photos during lessons, but the other pupils and the teacher also had the right to ask the two pupils to take a photograph of a certain situation. At the end of the narrative learning projects (examples of the projects are described in the next section), the teacher uploaded the photographs onto the school's intranet.

The pupils then did diamond ranking (e.g. Woolner et al, 2010; Clark, 2012; Woolner et al, 2012; Clark et al., 2013; Woolner et al, 2014) in pairs on PowerPoint slides for both projects. Pupils placed a photograph representing the most positive classroom practice on the first PowerPoint slide. They also placed photographs of the next two most positive classroom practices on the second slide. On the third slide, pupils placed photographs of practices that they rated as medium-level experiences during lessons. On the fourth slide, pupils placed two photographs of the classroom practices that were unimportant or uninteresting from their points of view. Finally, on the fifth slide, the teacher asked the pupils to place one photograph of the classroom practice that needed the most improvement. After creating these PowerPoint slides, pupils printed handouts (see Figure 1) and wrote narratives according to their rankings.

Pupils wrote the narratives anonymously. The teacher instructed the pupils to share their opinions and to give suggestions on how the teacher could improve those classroom practices that needed the most improvement. After the teacher had seen the diamonds and read through the children's narratives, she brought up this topic in the classroom.

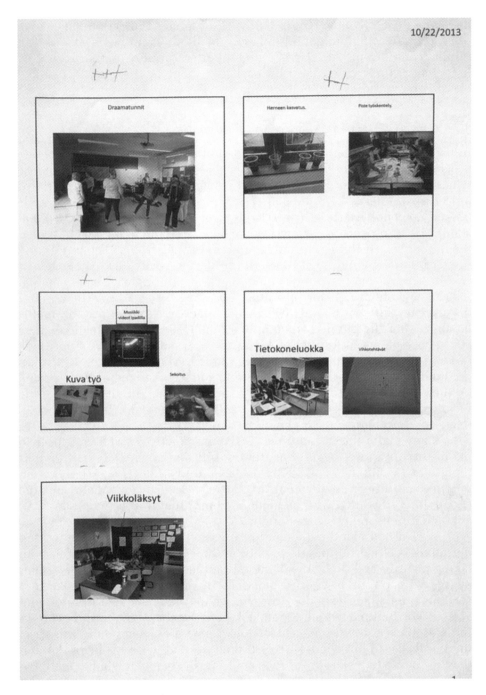

Figure 1. The diamond-ranking handout.

The pupils and the teacher discussed what to do regarding the issue that had been raised (Niemi, Kumpulainen & Lipponen, 2015a). In Case 1 we present how the diamond-ranking method can be seen as an implementation of Article 12: it supported pupils' participation by listening to their voices and by engaging them in the improvement of classroom practices and the development of teaching methods.

Case 1: Notebook Exercises in Mathematics

In the mathematics lessons, the teacher guided pupils as they completed tasks from the maths book. After those tasks, they were able to choose whether to challenge themselves and solve difficult problems in groups or to do extra pages from the maths book. In the diamond ranking, pupils ranked notebook exercises (twelve out of twenty-two) as the practice that should be improved. After the teacher had seen the diamonds and read the narratives, she brought up this topic in the classroom. The pupils and the teacher discussed what to do regarding the issue. For the teacher, it was important that the pupils completed tasks during each maths lesson instead of choosing, for example, drawing or reading. In a joint discussion, the pupils and the teacher made new rules for the maths lessons. After the pupils had completed the basic tasks in the book, they could choose one of four tasks: (1) to solve in pairs the book's notebook tasks in the lobby instead of working alone in the classroom; (2) to skip the notebook tasks in the book and try to solve a challenging task created by their teacher; (3) to plan a maths game or other activity on the topic for all the pupils to solve; or (4) to solve the tasks in the maths book (Niemi, Kumpulainen & Lipponen, 2015a).

Many claim that to improve classroom practices teachers appear to mainly accept those suggestions from pupils that are already part of their repertoire (McIntyre et al, 2005). Also, Lundy (2007) worries that in practice children's enjoyment of Article 12 is dependent on the cooperation of adults, who may not be committed to it or who may have a vested interest in not complying with it.

We learned that the diamond-ranking activity, together with written narratives, helped the pupils to choose their perspectives freely in both taking pictures and doing the diamond ranking. It also helped the teacher engage with pupils to change practices in the classroom and take into account pupils' suggestions. However, school is never free from official acts or curriculum, which create for both teachers and pupils certain limits to their ability to make decisions freely. For example, in this case, the pupils could not choose freely if they wanted to do maths or not, but they were free to make suggestions and improvements related to maths.

Lundy (2007) claims that adult concerns tend to fall into one of three groups: (1) scepticism about children's capacity to have meaningful input in decision making; (2) a worry that giving children more control will undermine authority; and finally, (3) concern that actions like this will require too much effort, which would be better spent on education itself.

Our findings present opposite outcomes: in this project, working with the photographs and doing the diamond rankings took about ninety minutes. It appeared to require little effort by the teacher and pupils. From the teacher's perspective, the activity level of the pupils in the maths lessons increased. When they had permission to choose one of the four options, the pupils completed more tasks in the lessons than they had before. Some pupils also started to score higher in maths tests – especially in problem-solving tasks – after the introduction of this new arrangement (Niemi, Kumpulainen, & Lipponen, 2015a).

Pupils' Participation in Building Wing Meetings

In Finland the Basic Education Act determines that the 'organization of pupil association activities shall be decided by the education provider. The organization of the association activities shall be informed by the age of the pupils and the local circumstances. Several schools or operational units may have a joint pupil association' (Basic Education Act 47 a § 2 (1267/2013), 1998).

For example, in the school mentioned in this study, there is a pupil association. Each classroom has chosen a representative and a deputy representative for the pupil association. The pupil association typically arranges a few activities during the school year. As Malone and Hartung (2010) and Baumfield et al (2013, p. 71) claim, too often these activities are relatively meaningless and tokenistic, with all the power remaining with the teacher and the school system, while pupils and teachers continue to face problems in their everyday life. Another problem with the pupil association is that it allows only a few pupils to join meetings and learn association procedures.

In everyday life pupils and teachers sharing the classes and lobbies in the smaller wings of the large school building confronted specific problems that only concerned a certain wing at a time. Those problems led three teachers of the school, including the first author of this chapter, to arrange building wing meetings for their pupils. The building wing meetings took place between 2012 and 2015. By the time of the meetings the pupils were between the fourth and sixth grades. In each meeting there were around seventy-five participants joining the meeting. In Case 2 we present how building wing meetings can be seen as an implementation of Article 12 by promoting pupils to make a difference collectively.

Case 2: Building Wing Meetings

The meetings' topics came from everyday life problems like football rules (e.g. who is allowed to join class teams); how to organise pupils' places in a school cafeteria; and how to affect the corridor's atmosphere by supporting constructive criticism and positive feedback. In most of the cases, teachers brought up the problems in the building wing meeting after hearing pupils' arguments or listening to pupils' disagreements with some rules.

In each meeting there was a chairperson and a secretary. The chairperson was either a pupil or a teacher. The secretary was a teacher. In each meeting the chairperson presented a problem, and the pupils suggested solutions. Each pupil had a right to make a suggestion or give a speech in order to support someone's suggestion. After discussion, pupils voted on the suggestions, and the idea that won the election was enacted. After the meeting a transcript was prepared by the secretary, signed by the secretary and the chairperson, and put on the wall of the corridor in order to show pupils what had been decided.

Discussions about children's rights under Article 12 often proceed with the assumption that there will always be some level of adult input (Lundy, 2007). That aspect occurred in the building wing meetings. In the beginning, adults initiated the meetings and brought the topics, but in the meetings the children solved the problems and shared their decisions with adults. In the case of wing meetings, the teachers did not complete a study of children's experiences, but they noticed that children took seriously decisions they had made, and they were dedicated, acting according to their own decisions.

As Hilppö et al (2015) have put it, many studies related to pupils' participation pay attention to the value of the reflexive aspect. In this study the focus was on tools to promote the pupils' aspirations. From that perspective, both the diamond-ranking method and building wing meetings worked well because they supported pupils' participation as both individuals and as collectives able to make a difference in their everyday practices in the classroom. Also, from the perspective of Hart's (1992), Shier's (2001) or Lundy's (2007) models, building wing meetings met the criteria set for participation. The meetings provided space and audience. Children were able to use their voices and put their decisions into action.

Supporting Pupils' Participation through Narrative Learning Projects

Article 13 states that a child shall have the right to freedom and to seek, receive and impart information and ideas of all kinds, regardless of frontiers, either orally, in writing or in print, in the form of art or through any other media of the child's choice (UNCRC). Despite that right, learning outcomes and children's assessment often take the form of written papers and tests.

In this study the teacher used narrative learning projects together with investigative learning in order to promote pupils' participation. The first through sixth grades were divided into four cross-curriculum projects according to themes set in the school curriculum for each grade. In each project, pupils worked in different groups; they worked alone, in pairs, in small groups or in a whole classroom group. The narratives created varied from scene plays, animation projects, and movies to self-written books or different kinds of art performances (e.g. window painting, making a model clay farm).

The theoretical background for narrative learning can be drawn from the basic statements of narrative research (e.g. Bruner 1986; Lieblich et al, 1998; Webster & Mertova, 2007) and Bruno Bettelheim's (1976) ideas. Narrative research notes that we are brought up surrounded by stories; they flow through us and ratify us from birth, telling us who we are and where we belong, what is right and what is wrong. In other words, narratives provide us with access to people's identity and personality (Lieblich et al, 1998, p. 7). Children are already clear about story structure. A child requires any story to be told to the end. Their imaginative play often displays continuous stories, and in their first writings they have a good grasp of structure. Furthermore, when small children describe their drawings or paintings, they will tell their story rather than describe the images (Bettelheim, 1976; Bolton, 2006).

Stories contain knowledge that is readily put into use in the world. Stories not only contain knowledge, but they can also be themselves the knowledge teachers want learners to possess (Webster & Mertova, 2007, p. 20). Stories also define relationships, a sequence of events, cause and effect, and a priority of items. These elements are likely to be remembered as a complex whole (Shaw et al, 1998, p. 42). As Richard Mitchell (1979) has said, 'Our knowledge is made up of the stories we can tell, stories that must be told in the language that we know ... Where we can tell no story, we have no knowledge' (see also Patton, 2002, p. 196).

In this study the focus in the learning projects was on developing pupils' skills for active, inquiry-based, reflective and communicative learning. Pupils investigated and solved problems via peer-led projects, and they were given opportunities to express the outcomes of their work in multiple narratives. From the perspective of the curriculum, learning activities were based on cross-curricular themes. The role of cross-curricular-themes, in the name of children's participation, is also stated often in the FNBE of 2014.

In the classroom, the lessons were formulated according to the following model, especially in project work:

1. Lessons begin with a question formulated by either the teacher or the pupils.
2. Pupils produce answers to the question according to their knowledge.
3. Pupils investigate the topic.
4. The answers and results are analysed and conceptualised together.
5. Assessment criteria are set.
6. Pupils create various learning narratives (Niemi, Kumpulainen & Lipponen, 2015b).

The next two cases present the implementation of these narrative projects in the second and fifth grades. The cases demonstrate the implementation of Article 13 by giving pupils the ability to express their learning in multiple ways.

Case 3: Energy-saving Project

At the beginning of the project, the second graders had 20 lessons (each lesson took 45 minutes) about energy. The pupils chose one toy, and they began to think of the materials used for the toy. They wrote the names of the materials on Post-it notes and added the notes to the sack (see Figure 2). Then they began to research each material one at a time and increased the number of concepts added to the sack. The pupils also investigated magazines targeted at children in order to learn how advertisements in magazines persuade children to buy new toys. They also researched where toys are made, how much energy is needed for transporting them to Finland, and where toys go after they are no longer used for play.

After those 20 lessons, each child wrote a movie script with the topic of saving energy. In their scripts, the eight-year-old pupils were able to include concepts about energy and reasons for energy consumption in their texts. For example, the pupils wrote the following:

> Once upon a time there was a granny, a girl and a boy who used a lot of energy. They had all the lights on, the TV was on; even the fridge was open. One day a man came from the energy company to tell them that they are wasting energy. The granny said: 'We use as much energy as we want to' ... Then the children stepped out and said: 'Thank you for letting us to know that. We will try to reduce the consumption of energy' ... Then their electricity was turned off ... The man from the energy company said that they could start by turning off all their electronic equipment ... The electricity came back on and the granny also learned that electricity is valuable.

After the scripts were ready, the pupils read their texts in groups. Each group chose one script, improved it together, and filmed it. Finally, there was a premiere of the movies in a classroom. Each movie received a peer evaluation and a teacher evaluation. In the evaluations, evaluators paid attention to the storyline and concepts learned in the lessons. Each child also completed a self-evaluation paper in which attention was paid to his or her own work and the group work.

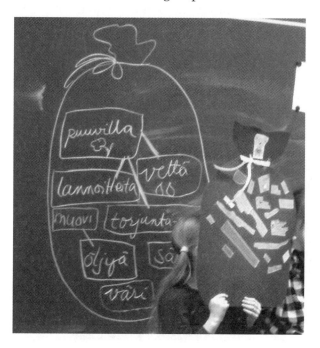

Figure 2. A material sack.

Case 4: Back to Ancient Rome Project

The project began with getting to know the history of Rome. The pupils studied historical knowledge in groups and added all concepts to the wall of ancient Rome in a classroom (see Figure 3).

Beginning with the first week of the project, each pupil wrote his or her own book, which concerned time travel to ancient Rome. Pupils were able to choose the perspective of the main character freely, and the main characters varied from a child to a fashion journalist and even a hamster. In the books, pupils looked at everyday life in ancient Rome through the eyes of the main character and compared the societies of ancient Rome and modern Finland.

After every week pupils were given a checklist of important concepts that had been studied together during the week. These concepts were supposed to be used in the books. At the end of the project, the concepts were once again collected in one evaluation form. Thus all pupils were aware of the assessment criteria, which they had participated in creating. During the project each pupil wrote a book with a minimum of four chapters. The pupils were also encouraged to draw pictures in their books. At the end of the project, the books were presented in a home/school evening. The pupils were able to choose the best part of their books and read them for the parents who attended the meeting.

Figure 3. The wall of ancient Rome in the classroom.

When examining these two examples from the perspective of either Hart's, Shier's or Lundy's model, one could say that the projects were curriculum (adult) initiated. It is worth asking if it is even possible for learning to always be child initiated because the goals are set in the curriculum. However, these examples show how learning projects can be organised so that pupils have an opportunity to express their own ideas and interpretations of the world in multiple ways. As Hart (1992) puts it, the sixth rung of the ladder is true participation because, though the projects at this level are initiated by adults, the decision making is shared with the young pupils.

Ethical Considerations

In action research the goal is to help people investigate reality in order to change it as well as change reality in order to investigate it (Kemmis & Wilkinson, 1998, p. 21). In literature, teacher research has often been considered a type of action research that should specifically incorporate reflective teaching and critical reflective practice (e.g. Lassonde & Israel, 2008, p. 7; Baumfield et al, 2013, p. 2). When doing action research study in a classroom, there are many ethical issues that have to be considered carefully (Zeni, 2013).

The ethical standard of responsibility – the special trust that the teacher-researcher has to exercise among pupils and their parents while investigating issues in the classroom – most clearly distinguishes action research. The challenge in planning action research is also to make the methods transparent (Zeni, 2013). In this study, the teacher-researcher presented the plan of the study for the parents in a parents' evening. The teacher-researcher asked each parent and child for permission regarding the parameters of the study – a practice the teacher-researcher repeated every year. After each action research cycle the teacher-researcher presented the results in a parents' evening and explained the new direction. Before publishing any papers, the parents had the opportunity to read the papers beforehand.

Zeni (2013, p. 258) claims that in action research full anonymity is almost impossible. For example, for this study it is easy to find out the identities of the children studied in the teacher-researcher's class. Also, children whose pictures are published in journals can be recognised. That's why the teacher-researcher first showed all pictures to be used in publications to the children and their parents and asked separate permission to use the pictures in the papers.

As Heikkinen et al (2007) maintain, research can never be ethically non-problematic, but researchers should be able to analytically approach ethical questions and propose solutions to them. Action research studies are problematic, but their strength relies on their strong connection to everyday practices. When teachers start to use daily practices as critical sites of inquiry, they position themselves as lifelong learners of how to improve school cultures (Cochran-Smith & Lytle, 2013).

Conclusions

In this chapter we have discussed how to enhance pupils' participation in educational practices in line with Articles 12 and 13 of the UNCRC. We have focused on reflecting the goals set for participation in the new national core curriculum for Finnish preschool and basic education (FNBE, 2014). In this chapter we also presented three models of participation – Roger Hart's (1992) ladder of participation, Harry Shier's (2001) model of the five levels of participation, and Laura Lundy's (2007) model for implementing Article 12 – and used these models as lenses when demonstrating how we enacted the curriculum goals for pupils' participation according to the FNBE (2014) in one classroom in Helsinki, Finland.

Previous researchers claim that too often participatory projects in schools do not lead to real change and action (Alderson, 2010). Teachers also often think that it is better to use their time on actual teaching than on pupils' participation (Lundy, 2007). In this study, building wing meetings and the diamond-ranking activity mostly supported pupils' participation. From the perspective of Hart's (1992), Shier's (2001) and Lundy's (2007) models, building wing meetings and the diamond-ranking activity met the criteria set for participation. The meeting provided space and an audience. Children were able to use their voices, and their decisions were put into action.

In this study the teacher used narrative learning projects in order to support pupils' participation in teaching and learning. The projects employed investigative learning in order to study concepts, and the presentation of learning outcomes took the form of various narratives. The teacher divided the goals set in the school curricula for each grade into four learning projects per year. When examining this outcome from the perspective of the models of participation, one could say that the projects were curriculum (adult) initiated, and they did not completely meet the criteria set for participation in those models. Narratives, however, gave pupils an opportunity to express their learning in multiple ways – pupils were able to use their imaginations and artistic elements in expressing their thinking. These are important issues in teaching and learning for the improvement of pupils' conceptual and methodological knowledge and skills for critical and creative thinking (FNBE, 2014, p. 29). Through narrative learning projects, pupils engaged in the process of creating assessment criteria.

When talking about pupils' participation in schools, one should remember that schools, just like life in general, are never free from curricula or official laws and acts. These limit teachers' and pupils' decision making. That is an aspect that is often left out of reflection when modelising participation. For example, in this study pupils could not choose freely if they wanted to do maths or not, but they were free to make suggestions and improvements related to maths lessons. Through narrative teaching and learning, the teacher was, nevertheless, able to provide pupils with a legitimate practice according to the sixth rung of participation. As Hart (1992) asserts, the sixth rung of the ladder describes true participation because, though the projects at this level are initiated by adults, the decision making is shared with the pupils.

Finnish educational policy respects children's rights, but it also respects the autonomy of teachers (e.g. Lanas & Kiilakoski, 2013). In Finland, teachers' work is not evaluated through national testing or school inspectors. Thus teachers can also pay attention to educational questions that do not relate directly to learning outcomes but that are important questions in pupils' everyday lives. For example, the building wing meetings and diamond-ranking activity were not part of any specific lessons, but the teacher was able to take time from teaching subjects to implement these practices. In this chapter we showed that these participatory activities did not take too much time from teaching and did not require too much effort for either the teacher or the pupils, but when pupils participated in improving the teaching methods and pedagogical activities of the classroom, their learning outcomes improved.

The examples presented in this chapter do not tell the whole truth of the state of pupils' participation in Finnish schools, as there is not much research on the topic in Finland. In many schools pupil participation takes the form of pupil associations and involving pupils in planning school festivals or different kinds of theme days. This chapter gives examples of how the national core curriculum for Finnish preschool and basic education has supported, now and in the past, the outcomes of Articles 12 and 13 of the UNCRC. In this chapter we have described how the goals concerning pupils' participation became lived practices in one classroom during a six-year period. We have also described how the forthcoming national core curriculum for Finnish preschool and basic education supports these goals. We hope that this chapter and the examples described inspire other educators – teachers and researchers – in other contexts to pay more attention to pupils' voices and participation in their classrooms in the future.

References

Alderson, P. (2010) Young Children's Individual Participation in 'All Matters Affecting the Child', in B. Percey-Smith & N. Thomas (Eds) *A Handbook of Children and Young People's Participation: perspectives from theory and practice*, pp. 88-96. Abingdon: Routledge.

Basic Education Act (1998). http://www.minedu.fi/OPM/Koulutus/koulutuspolitiikka/lait_ja_ohjeet/?lang=en (accessed 14 June 2015).

Baumfield, V., Hall, E. & Wall, K. (2013) *Action Research in Education*. London: SAGE.

Bettelheim, B. (1976) *The Uses of Enchantment*. London: Penguin. http://dx.doi.org/10.1037/e309842005-008

Bolton J. (2006) Narrative Writing: reflective enquiry into professional practice, *Educational Action Research*, 14(2), 202-218. http://dx.doi.org/10.1080/09650790600718076

Bruner, J. (1986) *Actual Minds, Possible Words*. Cambridge, MA: Harvard University Press.

Caine, V. (2010) Visualizing Community: understanding narrative inquiry as action research, *Educational Action Research*, 18(4), 481-496. http://dx.doi.org/10.1080/09650792.2010.524820

Carrington S., Bland, D & Brady, K. (2010) Training Young People as Researchers to Investigate Engagement and Disengagement in the Middle Years, *International Journal of Inclusive Education*, 14(5), 449-462. http://dx.doi.org/10.1080/13603110802504945

Clark, J. (2012) Using Diamond Ranking as Visual Cues to Engage Young People in the Research Process, *Qualitative Research Journal*, 12(2), 222-237. http://dx.doi.org/10.1108/14439881211248365

Clark, J., Laing, K., Tipaldy, L. et al (2013) *Making Connections: theory and practice of using visual methods to aid participation in research.* Newcastle upon Tyne: Research Centre for Learning and Teaching, Newcastle University.

Cochran-Smith, M. & Lytle, S.L. (2013) Teacher Research as Stance, in S. Noffke & B. Somekh (Eds) *The SAGE Handbook of Educational Action Research*, pp. 39-49. London: SAGE.

Fielding, M. (2007) Jean Rudduck (1937-2007) 'Carving a New Order of Experience': a preliminary appreciation of the work of Jean Rudduck in the field of student voice, *Educational Action Research*, 15(3), 323-336. http://dx.doi.org/10.1080/09650790701514234

FNBE (2014) The National Core Curriculum for Finnish Preschool and Basic Education. http://www.oph.fi/ops2016/perusteet (accessed 14 June 2015).

Frost, R. (2007) Developing the Skills of Seven- and Eight-year-old Researchers: a whole class approach, *Educational Action Research*, 15(3), 441-458. http://dx.doi.org/10.1080/09650790701514796

Gresalfi, M., Martin T., Hand, V. et al (2009) Constructing Competence: an analysis of student participation in the activity systems of mathematics classrooms, *Educational Studies in Mathematics*, 70(1), 49-70. http://dx.doi.org/10.1007/s10649-008-9141-5

Hart, R.A. (1992) Children's Participation, from Tokenism to Citizenship. UNICEF: Florence. http://www.unicef-irc.org/publications/pdf/childrens_participation.pdf (accessed 14 June 2015).

Heikkinen, H.L.T., Huttunen, R. & Syrjälä, L. (2007) Action Research as Narrative: five principles for validation, *Educational Action Research*, 15(1), 5-19. http://dx.doi.org/10.1080/09650790601150709

Hilppö, J., Lipponen, L., Kumpulainen, K. & Virlander, M. (2015) Sense of Agency and Everyday Life: children's perspective, *Learning, Culture and Social Interaction.* http://dx.doi.org/10.1016/j.lcsi.2015.10.001

Kemmis, S. & Wilkinson, M. (1998) Participatory Action Research and the Study of Practice, in B. Atweh, S. Kemmis & P. Weeks (Eds) *Action Research in Practice: partnerships for social justice in education*, pp. 21-36. London: Routledge.

Kiilakoski, T., Gretschel, A. & Nivala, E. (2012) Osallisuus, kansalaisuus, hyvinvointi [Participation, citizenship, wellbeing], in A. Gretschel & T. Kiilakoski (Eds) *Demokratiakasvatus* [Democracy education]. Nuorisotutkimusseuran julkaisuja, 118, pp. 9-33. Helsinki: Nuorisotutkimusseura.

Lanas, M. & Kiilakoski, T. (2013) Growing Pains: teacher becoming a transformative agent, *Pedagogy, Culture and Society*, 21(3), 343-360. http://dx.doi.org/10.1080/14681366.2012.759134

Lansdown, G. (2010) The Realisation of Children's Participation Rights: critical reflections, in B. Percey-Smith & N. Thomas (Eds) *A Handbook of Children and Young People's Participation: perspectives from theory and practice*, pp. 11-23. Abingdon: Routledge.

Lassonde, C.A. & Israel, S.E. (2008) *Teachers Thinking Action*. Newark, DE: International Reading Association.

Lieblich, A., Tuval-Mashiach, R. & Zilber, T. (1998) *Narrative Research: reading, analysis, and interpretation*. Applied Social Research Methods Series, vol. 47. Thousand Oaks, CA: SAGE.

Lundy, L. (2007) 'Voice' Is Not Enough: conceptualising Article 12 of the United Nations Convention on the Rights of the Child, *British Educational Research Journal*, 33(6), 927-942. http://dx.doi.org/10.1080/01411920701657033

Malone, K. & Hartung, C. (2010) Challenges of Participatory Practices with Children, in B. Percey-Smith & N. Thomas (Eds) *A Handbook of Children and Young People's Participation: perspectives from theory and practice*, pp. 24-38. Abingdon: Routledge.

Mcintyre, D., Pedder, D. & Rudduck, J. (2005) Pupil Voice: comfortable and uncomfortable learning for teachers, *Research Papers in Education*, 20(2), 149-168. http://dx.doi.org/10.1080/02671520500077970

Messiou, K. (2011) Collaborating with Children in Exploring Marginalisation: an approach to inclusive education, *International Journal of Inclusive Education*, 16(12), 1311-1322. http://dx.doi.org/10.1080/13603116.2011.572188

Mitchell, R. (1979) *Less than Words Can Say: the underground grammarian*. Boston, MA: Little, Brown.

Niemi, R., Kumpulainen, K. & Lipponen, L. (2015a) Pupils as Active Participants: diamond ranking as a tool to investigate pupils' experiences of classroom practices, *European Educational Research Journal*. http://dx.doi.org/10.1177/1474904115571797

Niemi, R., Kumpulainen, K. & Lipponen, L (2015b) Pupils' Documentation Enlightening Teachers' Practical Theory and Pedagogical Actions, *Educational Action Research*, 23(4), 599-614. http://dx.doi.org/10.1080/09650792.2014.942334

Niemi, R., Kumpulainen, K., Lipponen, L. & Hilppö, J.A. (2015) Pupils' Perspectives on the Lived Pedagogy of the Classroom, *Education 3-13*, 43(6), 681-697.

Patton, M.Q. (2002) *Qualitative Research & Evaluation Methods*, 3rd edn. Thousand Oaks, CA: SAGE.

Shaw, G., Brown, R. & Bromiley P. (1998) Strategic Stories: how 3M is rewriting business planning, *Harvard Business Review*, 76(3), 41-50.

Shier, H. (2001) Pathways to Participation: openings, opportunities and obligations. A New Model for Enhancing Children's Participation in

Decision-making, in Line with Article 12.1 of the United Nations Convention of the Right of the Child, *Children and Society*, 15, 107-117. http://dx.doi.org/10.1002/chi.617

Tangen, R. (2009) Conceptualising Quality of School Life from Pupils' Perspectives: a four-dimensional model, *International Journal of Inclusive Education*, 13(8), 829-844. http://dx.doi.org/10.1080/13603110802155649

Thomas, N. (2007) Towards a Theory of Children's Participation, *International Journal of Children's Rights*, 15, 199-218. http://dx.doi.org/10.1163/092755607X206489

United Nations Convention on the Rights of the Child (UNCRC) (1989) UN General Assembly Resolution 44/25. http://www.ohchr.org/EN/ProfessionalInterest/Pages/CRC.aspx (accessed 4 January 2016).

Webster, L. & Mertova, P. (2007) *Using Narrative Inquiry as a Research Method: an introduction to using critical event narrative analysis in research on learning and teaching.* London: Routledge.

Woolner, P., Clark, J., Hall, E. et al (2010) Pictures Are Necessary But Not Sufficient: using a range of visual methods to engage users about school design, *Learning Environments Research*, 13(1), 1-22. http://dx.doi.org/10.1007/s10984-009-9067-6

Woolner, P., Clark, J., Laing, K. et al (2012) Changing Spaces: preparing students and teachers for a new learning environment, *Children, Youth and Environments*, 22(1), 52-74. http://dx.doi.org/10.7721/chilyoutenvi.22.1.0052

Woolner, P., Clark, J., Laing, K. et al (2014) A School Tries to Change: how leaders and teachers understand changes to space and practices in a UK secondary school, *Improving Schools*, 17(2), 148-162. http://dx.doi.org/10.1177/1365480214537931

Zeni, J. (2013) Ethics and the 'Personal' in Action Research, in S. Noffke & B. Somekh (Eds) *The SAGE Handbook of Educational Action Research*, pp. 254-266. London: SAGE.

CHAPTER 5

Children's Rights in Times of Austerity: social awareness of pre-service teachers in Portugal

JOANA LÚCIO & FERNANDO ILÍDIO FERREIRA

SUMMARY From 2010 – and particularly after 2011, with the coming into force of the Financial Adjustment Programme – Portugal's economic and financial situation worsened with the adoption of a set of austerity measures that have had, and continue to have, a direct impact on families' well-being, and therefore on that of children, especially in terms of access to health care, education and social support from the State. According to EUROSTAT data, as of 2011, 28.6% of Portuguese children were at risk of poverty and social exclusion. In this chapter, the authors discuss the issue of children's rights in a context of social and economic cutbacks, according to three dimensions – provision, protection and participation – analysing how children's right to citizenship and civic engagement can become impaired in times of precariousness and social vulnerability. To this effect, they assess pre-service teachers' perceptions about their role (and the school's role) as a platform for children's civic and political development, while also discussing the transformations operated at the university by the Bologna Process, which has shown a tendency to saturate teacher training curricula with didactics-related content, to the detriment of issues such as personal and social development, and children's participation.

An Introduction to Portugal's Situation in the Context of the Global Recession

The late 2000s were witness to the start of a period of general economic decline that the International Monetary Fund (IMF), in its April 2009 'World Economic Outlook' report, dubbed the worst global recession since World War II (International Monetary Fund, 2009). The scale and timing of this recession varied from country to country: while the United

States' National Bureau of Economic Research considers that the US recession extended over a period of only 18 months, from December 2007 to June 2009 (National Bureau of Economic Research, 2010), the impact of this crisis at the European level was, and still is, felt at various degrees.

In Portugal, the economic crisis began to take shape before 2008, after several years of low growth. A drop in tax revenues, followed by a rise in government debt (Eurostat, 2013a,b), finally led, in 2011, to a request for financial assistance from the European Commission, the European Central Bank and the IMF (known as the 'troika').

While the omnipresent notion of 'austerity' – understood as a set of policy measures established with the purpose of reducing government budget deficits – emerges roughly at the time of the coming into force of the Financial Adjustment Programme, prior to that (*circa* 2009) a range of responses were introduced, such as reductions in unemployment assistance, public-sector pay cuts, reductions in numbers of public service workers and increases in consumption taxes and social contributions. While some countries (such as Greece and Spain) have, over time, abolished some of the measures initially included in their economic consolidation plans that had more direct implications on child well-being (e.g. birth grants, paid parental leave, tax reductions for families with more children), others have continued to restrict or fully suppress access to family or child benefits. In Portugal, such measures have included reversals of education allowance extension, income ceiling lowered and more frequent assessments to reduce overpayments (Martorano, 2014). According to data published by the European Anti-Poverty Network (EAPN, 2014), the weight of health and social protection expenses, in Portugal, currently represents less than half of total public expenditure.

According to Caritas Europa's Crisis Monitoring Report from 2014, with 27.4% of the population considered to be at risk for poverty and/or social exclusion, in Portugal, the risk-of-poverty rate for children is 31.6% (Leahy et al, 2014). As noted in the Innocenti Report Card 12, 'in countries where the Great Recession hit hardest, children are suffering the most and will bear the consequences the longest' (UNICEF Office of Research, 2014, p. 14). According to this report, the effective child poverty rate, in Portugal, increased 1% between 2008 and 2012. The report also places Portugal among those countries most affected by the so-called Great Recession, as one of the countries with evident fiscal problems that experienced market pressure.

'Two factors prove particularly important for households with children: the position of parents in the labour market and the depleted capacity of states to protect families' (UNICEF Office of Research, 2014, p. 14). Within this framework, this chapter will present an analysis of the issue of children's rights in a context of economic austerity according to three dimensions, invoking the three categories of rights of the United Nations Convention on the Rights of the Child (UNCRC): provision (in which we will examine the Portuguese welfare state from a socio-historical perspective); protection (in which we will analyse the nature and the impact of spending cuts in state-based social support); and participation (in which we will discuss how financial and economic fragility can undermine or even suspend concerns with citizenship and social engagement rights). To support the analysis of the latter, this chapter draws upon the perceptions of pre-service teachers of their experiences during practicum, collected via written narratives, as part of a wider research project aimed at investigating the components of the curriculum of initial teacher education (ITE), particularly in regard to the social and cultural aspects of teaching.

While it is an analysis of teachers and schools as platforms for the civic and political development (and engagement) of children, this chapter is also a discussion of how the Bologna Process has transformed ITE programmes, in the context of a praxiological tendency for an attachment to a more scholarly model, to the detriment of dimensions such as social awareness/consciousness and participation. Finally, it is also a contribution to the sociology of childhood, rooted in the understanding of children as competent social actors, and presenting a critical analysis of how austerity programmes impact on these young citizens' rights and their ability to participate.

Beginning with a socio-economic and historical framing, moving on to an assessment of the current situation in terms of pre-service teacher's views on children's rights, and concluding with a reference to the new (as of November 2015) political situation in Portugal, this chapter is built on a chronological progression (past, present and future) that mirrors the book's global orientation.

The Portuguese Welfare State: a contextualisation

Historically, the first motions leading up to the creation of a welfare state in Portugal date from the early twentieth century, prior to the implementation of the Republican regime, with the development of the mutualistic movement and the creation of several organisations of a social nature, and later the legislation of mandatory social insurance for support in case of illness, workplace accidents, disability, old age and orphanhood/widowhood.

However, it was not until the 'Estado Novo' [1] period, and mainly after 1935 (with the approval of the Basic Law of Welfare Organisation [2]), that Portugal became a part of a broader, European-level movement favouring state-based intervention in the social field. While the dictatorial regime is consensually considered to have imposed severe limitations, or even full restrictions, upon many areas of civic and political participation, several authors have analysed how social policies evolved during the '*Estado Novo*', noting how it contributed to the establishment of the foundations of a true welfare state, as uniform and standardised social security progressively replaced the voluntarism of a beneficence- (or charity-) based system (Cardoso & Rocha, 2003; Pereirinha & Carolo, 2009).

In the period following World War II, and given a relative stability in the number of active beneficiaries, there was, up until the 1960s, a progressive broadening of the welfare coverage – namely, in terms of access to health care (with the creation of socio-medical services) and the creation of the family allowance ('*abono de família*'). A new reform in 1962 established a general social security scheme. In 1969 [3], other gaps in the social protection system were filled – namely, for workers outside the regular job market (such as agricultural workers), as well as other specific occupations (e.g. hairdressers, day-labourers and especially household workers). While this expansion in coverage did not always correspond to an increase in the value of the benefits, it did contribute to a steady growth in the State's expenses in connection with social support, especially between 1971 and 1974, when the annual growth rate was 35-37% (Pereirinha & Carolo, 2009).

After 1974, other relevant changes were implemented concerning the social role of the State – namely, the creation of the unemployment allowance (1975) and the establishment of social pensions on a non-contributive basis (1977). In 1979, the provisional government then led by Maria de Lourdes Pintassilgo issued the Decree-Law no. 513/79 which established the minimum social protection scheme, including: social pension; supplementary pension for the seriously disabled; orphan's pension; family allowance; monthly allowance for disabled minors; and social facilities (Pereirinha & Carolo, 2009).

The early 1980s was a period of expenditure restraint in social security, with an increase in warranty periods for old age pensions, as well as some transformations in the regime of social protections for agricultural workers. The year of 1986 marks a turning point, as the beginning of a new phase in the growth rhythm of the State's social expenditure that also coincided with Portugal joining what was then called the European Economic Community (EEC). By that time, public social expenditure was around 8% of the national gross domestic product (GDP) (Pereirinha & Carolo, 2009); that number grew steadily, markedly after 1990. While the investment in health care, in convergence with the European tendency, was one of the main contributors to the increase in state expenditure, after 1990, the most relevant aspect was the increase in expenses in connection with old age pensions.

While it is undeniable that the first decade of EEC membership corresponded to significant improvements in terms of infrastructures and several social indicators, this did not mean the definite extinction of social injustice and inequalities; what it did, according to Estanque (2012), was foster illusions about a state with unlimited resources, while necessary structural reforms were continuously postponed. One area that saw relevant restructuring, however, was that of public employment, which had been long acknowledged as one of the main causes for the worsening of public expenditure and its deficit (Estanque, 2012). This much-needed restructuring was one of the main justifications behind an ample set of measures (adopted by recent governments) aimed at reforming the state, a concern made more pressing with the progression of the economic crisis.

It is worth noting that one relevant aspect of the Portuguese context, in terms of the State's social responsibilities, is the influence of what has been dubbed the 'solidarity economy' (Ramos, 2011; Estanque, 2012). Also known as the 'third sector', this dynamic has sought to minimise the gaps in the State's role as provider. Cooperatives and citizens' associations, particularly, have had and continue to have a significant role in meeting families' needs regarding childcare (e.g. nursery/crèche provision and after-school activities) and support for the elderly (e.g. day care facilities, occupational therapy and home care services).

Economic Crisis and Austerity Measures:
the effects on families and children

According to UNICEF's assessment of the subjective impact of the economic crisis on households with children, in 17 European countries, 'perceived impact was greater on average for respondents with children ... (48%) than for those without children (34%).... the presence of at least one child ... significantly increased the probability of reporting an impact of the crisis' (Chzhen, 2014, p. 10).

In Portugal, the implementation of austerity measures – especially following the Memorandum of Understanding signed between the Portuguese government and the 'troika' in 2011 – has led to a progressive worsening of families' living conditions and to an increase in poverty. Between 2010 and 2013, the State's economic support for families was significantly reduced: access to welfare benefits such as the family allowance, support for education-related expenses, parental leave allowances, unconditional basic income and unemployment allowances was frankly restricted, not only in terms of the number of benefiting families, but also in terms of the benefits' value (Grilo, 2013). In terms of facilities and services, after a significant growth between 2006 and 2011 [4], since 2011 there has been virtually no investment in the broadening of the pre-school network. The strategy has been to maximise the capacity of the existing facilities (increasing the legal threshold of children per classroom), which has obvious impacts on the quality of childcare services, and even on the children's safety and well-being.

According to Eurostat data, '27% of children within EU-27 were at risk for poverty or social exclusion in 2011. In Portugal, that number amounted to 28.6%' (Grilo, 2013, p. 13). According to Grilo (2013), an individual is considered to be at risk for poverty or social exclusion when at least one of the following conditions is verified: monetary poverty, low labour intensity within the family or severe material deprivation.

Eurostat data published in June 2015 indicate that Portugal currently has the fifth highest unemployment rate in the European Union (EU) – increasing from 7.6% in 2008 to 13.2% in 2015 – and the fourth highest youth unemployment rate (33.3% in 2015). Among other austerity policies, the Portuguese government cut public-sector wages, increased taxes and slashed spending on social welfare programmes that provided social security benefits. These austerity measures were adopted as part of a broader goal to reduce the deficit below 5.9%. Although successful in reducing the deficit, this austerity has had a significant impact on the Portuguese workers' status.

Between 2008 and 2012, the proportion of children up to the age of 17 living in jobless households nearly doubled in Portugal and Spain (UNICEF Office of Research, 2014). The percentage of children experiencing severe material deprivation has been systematically increasing since 2008; in 2011 that number was 11.3% (Grilo, 2013).

The progressive worsening of the country's economic situation can also be assessed in terms of how many families are requesting humanitarian aid: demands on the services of Caritas Portugal, for example, almost doubled between 2011 and 2012, bringing the number of families that have requested some sort of support up to 56,000 (Leahy et al, 2014). According to this same report, 'the High Commissioner for Human Rights of the Council of Europe has identified Portugal as amongst the European countries where, as a result of austerity measures, there is a risk of a rise in children engaged in child labour' (Leahy et al, 2014, p. 55).

Portugal is also cited in an editorial in the *British Medical Journal* relating to the negative impacts on access to health care resulting from the economic crisis and austerity packages: while the hospitals (and other health care facilities) themselves suffer from budgetary cuts that have an influence on the overall quality of services, people in poverty are also more likely to defer medical expenses (Leahy et al, 2014).

Concomitantly, 'massive reductions in the education budget in recent years are a potentially extremely damaging trend …, given that Portugal already performs badly in important indicators such as early school leaving' (Leahy et al, 2014, p. 55). According to Benavente et al (2014), this is the situation in the education sector after 2011: (i) an increasing number of pupils per class; (ii) the re-introduction of national exams in all levels of schooling (with a growing number of students being guided towards vocational programmes); (iii) an increase in teachers' workload; and (iv) the disappearance of certain components of the curriculum and the suppression (or reduction) of additional tutoring in schools, both resulting in a growing number of teachers being dispensed with. Nowadays, schools and teachers have to respond not only to the purpose of educating children, but also to issues arising from the transformations resulting from austerity in the lives of students and their families. In the context of the *Programa de Emergência Alimentar* [5], hundreds of social canteens were created across the country, in cooperation with social solidarity institutions. In the first semester of 2015, approximately 8.6 million meals were served. Resulting from partnerships involving local governments, other local organisations and parents' associations, canteens within the schools have also been kept functioning during holiday periods, so as to ensure that children have access to at least one hot meal per day.

Children's Rights: fragile economy, fragile citizenship

The economic recession has had obvious impacts on families' most basic needs, and those of their children: less disposable income means restricted access to food, proper housing, health care, etc. However, there are other, more subtle impacts – namely, in terms of a sense of security and a positive general outlook on life: 'children feel anxious and stressed when parents endure unemployment or income loss, and they suffer family downturns in subtle and painfully evident ways' (UNICEF Office of Research, 2014, p. 2).

Twenty-five years after the UNCRC [6] was internationally recognised, many of its commitments remain unrealised, and the Great Recession – affecting developed countries seen as the most capable of delivering on them – has once again put children all across Europe (and the world) in a critical position, where their basic rights are questioned.

In its 2014 report regarding the Portuguese situation, the Committee on the Rights of the Child notes that 'the recession and the current financial and economic crisis are taking their toll on families and on public social investment, including on the prospects of implementing the Convention', by 'increasing the risk of children being exposed to poverty and affecting the enjoyment of many of the rights contained in the Convention, including health, education and social protection' (United Nations, 2014, p. 3).

This report also sheds some light on the issue of training in human rights and children's rights: the Committee expresses its concern regarding how such training opportunities/initiatives may have 'been negatively impacted by budget cuts due to the financial crisis, and ... [do] not reach all levels of society, including children and professionals working with or for children' (United Nations, 2014, p. 6).

In terms of the respect for the views of the child [7], the Committee states its concern that efforts to ensure respect for the views of the child are not being adequately implemented in all relevant areas – namely, 'regarding the education system and its reform' (United Nations, 2014, p. 8). Likewise, as the Committee notes, professionals working with and for children are not receiving adequate training regarding the right of the child to be heard. The views of children are seen as particularly relevant for the evaluation of the education system, to determine the reasons behind high drop-out and repetition rates.

The child's right to participation, in its many forms, is explicitly acknowledged in the UNCRC's Article 23 (where it is stated that children with disabilities should be awarded conditions that facilitate their active participation in the community) and Article 31 (which recognises the child's right to participate freely and fully in the cultural and artistic life of their community). It is worth mentioning that 'the acknowledgement of children's right to participate is indelibly connected not only to an acknowledgement of their ability and willingness to do so, but also to their recognition as actors in their own right' (Lúcio & I'Anson, 2015, p. 131).

In their discussion about the participation of children in democratic processes in kindergarten, Danner and Jonyniene (2012) note that such experiences, at a young age, have an educational purpose insofar as children are given the opportunity to learn about rights and duties through their empirical exercise, contributing to a better understanding about the limits to their freedom, as citizens, through an awareness of the effects of their own actions in relation to their peers.

In 2013, the European Commission (EC) issued a recommendation regarding the organisation and implementation of policies to address child poverty and social exclusion, and to promote children's well-being (European Commission, 2013). According to the EC's recommendation, one of the core aspects for the development of adequate strategies is the acknowledgement of the influence children have over their own well-being, and of their resilience in overcoming adverse situations. Therefore, not only should children be offered opportunities to participate in informal learning activities that take place outside the home and after regular school hours, they should also be enabled and encouraged to express their views in decision-making processes that affect their lives. According to this recommendation, professionals working with and for children should be encouraged (and trained) to actively involve them.

With these concerns and recommendations in mind, it bears discussing how Portuguese schools and teachers are integrating the issue of children's rights in their daily lives, in times of austerity, and how pre-service teachers (as, simultaneously, insiders and outsiders in the context of schools) assess the present and outline the future.

Assessing Social Awareness of
Pre-service Teachers: methodological issues

Currently, in Portugal, teacher training for both pre-school and basic education levels (first and second cycles, until the age of 12) confers a master's degree, following upon a three-year licentiate degree in basic education. Before Bologna, the duration and number of European Credit Transfer and Accumulation System (ECTS) credits were the same for pre-school education and all other levels of schooling, but then the situation changed: the current duration of the master's degree in pre-school education is two semesters (corresponding to 60 ECTS credits), with a practicum taking place during the second semester (worth 30 ECTS credits); the master's degree in pre-school and elementary education is three semesters long (90 ECTS units), with a practicum happening during the second and third semesters (worth 45 ECTS units); the master's degree in elementary and middle education is four semesters long (120 ECTS credits), with a practicum during the third and fourth semesters (worth 55 ECTS credits). The licentiate degree in basic education (from which the vast majority of students enrolling in these master's degrees stem) has also experienced a reduction in the amount of time devoted to practicum: of the degree's 180 ECTS credits (six semesters), only 20 of them correspond to an introduction to professional practice, distributed between four course units (CUs), across different semesters. Not only that, but the already limited number of practicum-oriented hours are mainly occupied with classes (at the university), with very little time actually spent in schools. This is relevant evidence of a certain devaluation of pre-school and basic education ITE, in clear contradiction of the fundamental importance of the early years in a child's education and overall development.

This chapter draws upon data collected in the context of a wider research project, aimed at investigating components of the curriculum of ITE, particularly in regard to the social and cultural aspects of teaching. Student (or pre-service) teachers enrolled in ITE programmes were invited to participate in the project. In total, 18 volunteered, all females, ages ranging between 21 and 24. They were enrolled in the master's degree in pre-school education ($n = 11$) or the master's degree in pre-school and elementary education ($n = 7$).

To gain initial access to the field and a group of participants, the research group contacted the directors of the two master's degrees, asking for their cooperation. After accessing a list of email addresses (of individual students and each class delegate), potential participants were sent information on the project and asked to contribute with their written narratives, based on an attached script. The collaborating directors were asked to promote the participation of their students, during class. Participants who had not had the opportunity to send their narratives were invited to write theirs during the annual end-of-the-year seminar. Data collection was completed in May 2015.

Subjects were asked to build a written narrative about their field experiences during practicum, in schools. To aid in the construction of these narratives, participants were given a script including a set of questions aimed at exploring their beliefs, conceptions and practices. The script included descriptive questions (related to specific experiences, situations, phenomena, things that the students had learned in the schools, kindergartens and day care centres), reflexive questions (pertaining to how these experiences had contributed to their training) and purposeful questions (the students' own suggestions/proposals regarding ITE curricula, considering the contexts they had observed and how they perceive their curriculum to correspond to the reality at hand).

Data analysis was done in two stages: first, a vertical analysis (Miles & Huberman, 1994), during which each participant's contribution was analysed individually; second, a comparative (or horizontal) cross-case analysis (Miles & Huberman, 1994), during which the method of 'constant comparative analysis' (Glaser & Strauss, 1967) was used in search of commonalities, as well as dissimilarities.

In this chapter, our discussion will fall upon participants' discourses concerning the wider concept of children's rights, but also the issue of children's participation – and how it is put into practice in the contexts where the practicum took place – and the schools' role in promoting children's well-being and social engagement.

The value of written narratives lies in how they provide participants with the opportunity to look back on their learning experiences, all the while raising self- and hetero-awareness, promoting reflection on beliefs and implicit theories, and aiding with the process of making sense of one's own experience (Elliott, 2005). Through narrative accounts, people are invited to look back on specific moments or situations, and learn from them through a process of meaning making (Hollway & Jefferson, 2000; Elliott, 2005), which is particularly relevant within the context of ITE – namely, after practicum, in the case of this study. Issues of time and space, and their relation to the social context (Clandinin et al, 2007), are vital in this regard.

The Bologna Process and the
Changes in ITE Programmes in Portugal

Within a context of policy changes and complex and increasingly demanding expectations put onto schools and teachers (namely, as many families' ability to cater to their children's most basic needs is put into question), it is important to understand how ITE is corresponding to these challenges, particularly in what concerns practicum, and taking into consideration these pre-service teachers' perspectives.

Like many other European countries, Portugal has undergone a restructuring process of ITE programmes, as a result of the implementation of the Bologna Process. Decree-Law no. 43/2007 determined the basic professional qualifications for teaching (from pre-school to secondary education), and is based on a number of identified key elements in the restructuring process: (i) the need for a higher professional qualification for teachers (at a second-cycle level, i.e. a master's degree); (ii) a curriculum based on learning outcomes related to teacher performance; (iii) a research-based qualification; (iv) the importance of practicum (i.e. the observation and collaboration in actual teaching situations, under the supervision of a certified and experienced mentor); (v) school-university partnerships; and (vi) the quality assurance of teachers' qualification and of ITE. Following the implementation of these changes in ITE curricula, in order to become a teacher, a three-year (licentiate) degree is needed, necessarily followed by a master's degree in teaching (usually a two-year programme). There is, then, an implied separation between first-cycle-level training and second-cycle-level training (with the latter, the master's degree, necessarily being in the field of ITE). More recently, Decree-Law no. 79/2014 established a new framework for ITE in Portugal, including the following curriculum components: (i) training in a specific subject matter; (ii) general educational training; (iii) specific didactics (for a given level of teaching and subject matter); (iv) cultural, social and ethical education; and (v) professional practice. However, the component of cultural, social and ethical education awards no actual ECTS credits.

This new configuration – a 'consecutive model' – has been seen as a drawback in relation to previous models of teacher education (i.e. the so-called integrated model, which included 4-5 years of (licentiate-level) training, during which student teachers would benefit from training in educational sciences and a specific subject matter simultaneously, plus one year of practicum). The new model, based on a more fragmented study programme/curriculum, split into semester-long CUs (sub-divided, for their part, into modules), emphasises subject-specific knowledge and didactics, while a significant part of practicum is brought back into the universities, and away from schools. This 'academisation' of ITE curricula shifts the focus away from the student teacher's practical skills, lending more relevance to how they perform academically (Ek et al, 2013).

It is also noteworthy that the research component, evident in the previous legal framework for ITE programmes, is absent in the aftermath of the Bologna Process. All in all, recent policy changes have undermined the possibility to put the necessary emphasis on the wider social and cultural contexts in which pre-service teachers will eventually work.

The issue of children's rights can be seen, in post-Bologna ITE programmes, as a transversal – albeit mostly implicit – issue: whether or not it is explicitly addressed during pre-service teachers' training depends more on the faculty's sensibility towards the theme, and its relevance for a particular CU's syllabus, and less on it being a key element in the curricula. At the University of Minho, where this study was conducted, the licentiate degree in basic education is strong in didactics-related CUs (such as mathematics, geography, linguistics, biology, arts, history, etc.), while CUs pertaining to the areas of general education and professional practice (such as pedagogy of childhood, developmental psychology, sociology of childhood and education, curricular development, etc.) make up only 35 of the degree's 180 ECTS credits. Neither the master's degree in pre-school education nor the master's degree in pre-school and elementary education (in which the participants in this study were enrolled) includes any CUs explicitly dealing with the issues of children's participation or citizenship – while, for example, the master's degree in education (more oriented towards adult and community education) includes a CU on education for autonomy and participation (worth 6 of 120 ECTS credits), and the master's degree in teaching in elementary and middle education includes two optional CUs (each worth 5 of 120 ECTS credits) relevant for this theme: personal development and social interaction, and education and citizenship.

Pre-service Teachers' Views on Children's Rights, Participation and the Social Role of the School

When asked about their knowledge regarding the issue of *children's rights*, all participants mentioned having experienced more or less explicit learning opportunities, both prior to and during their enrolment in the ITE programmes. One participant, for example, states that 'I obtained this knowledge during Secondary Education and revisited it during the Licentiate degree in Education' (excerpt from one of the narratives). Some participants name specific CUs in the context of which the issue of children's rights was approached (namely, sociology of childhood), while others identify this as a more transversal content in their curriculum. One participant goes as far as to state that 'every teacher [I have had], from Pre-school up to the Master's degree, has shown a concern with talking about these rights' (excerpt from one of the narratives). Extra-curricular events, such as conferences and seminars – both those taking place at the university where the participants are enrolled, and those that they autonomously seek and attend – are also listed as having contributed to the participants' training on the issue of children's rights. One participant points out how they extended their knowledge about children's rights while developing further readings to support the construction of their pedagogical intervention project (a type of essay written by the student teachers prior to the start of their practicum, in which they plan their future activities at the schools).

As far as what children's rights are – i.e. what rights do children actually hold – participants explicitly mention the right to education, the right to being respected, the right to having a family, the right to food, the right to play, the right to well-being and the right to participating in decision-making processes that concern them.

For some participants, the issue of children's rights is inextricably connected with the UNCRC: for example, one participant states that '[children's rights] are a set of rules that present to us which rights and needs each child has and deserves' (excerpt from one of the narratives). Other participants mention their knowledge about the existence of the Convention: one participant states that 'there is a referential listing these rights' (excerpt from one of the narratives), while another states that the UNCRC has evolved over time.[8]

At least one participant mentions not having had any explicit contact with the issue of children's rights during ITE, while another refers to having experienced only a brief (and insufficient) approach to the subject.

As far as *children's participation* is concerned, the vast majority of participants claim to have experienced explicit instances of children's participation during their practicum. Nonetheless, quite a few of them mention that children's participation is not fostered in all schools. One participant distinguishes between the context of the crèche and the context of the kindergarten, stating that, in the former, children's contribution for the scheduling of their activities and their overall participation in terms of decision-making was more limited. Another participant views this as something that depends less on the context and more on the teacher: 'It depends: some kindergarten teachers allow that participation, others don't' (excerpt from one of the narratives). One participant notes that when it came to determining a list of possible activities, the children had no right to choose which they preferred. Another participant notes that the teacher's views (and choices) prevail in the majority of situations.

In terms of how exactly the children participate, in the contexts where the participants developed their practicum, voting (inside the classroom) was one of the identified strategies for the promotion of participation. In some of the contexts, children also offer their opinion on current and possible (future) activities, while, in others, they are identified as actively participating during the welcome period (at the beginning of the school day). Two participants refer to how children participate in day-to-day school routines (although these are not specified). For some participants, however, there seems to be some confusion between children's participation and free (or undirected) play;

one participant, in particular, states that children are allowed to 'participate freely in work areas' (excerpt from one of the narratives), meaning that the child is allowed to choose which activities they would like to undertake, but they do not have a say, for example, in the decision-making process leading up to the list of possible activities.

Children's participation is, for some participants, related to autonomous (or child-led) learning. Reflecting upon their intervention in the classroom, one participant states that 'I myself chose to let the children participate and build their learning by themselves. In the evaluation activity, they led me, and in the discovery of geometric solids, the children performed the experiments' (excerpt from one of the narratives). To this same extent, at least one other participant mentions that 'children had a voice and a turn; it was a constant concern on my part' (excerpt from one of the narratives). Another participant mentions that 'the right to participation is practised at the institution, given that the child is at the centre of the learning process and that all the teachers correspond to each and every child's interests and needs' (excerpt from one of the narratives).

Participation is also strongly associated with engagement and motivation. One participant points out how the teacher they observed made an explicit effort to equally involve all children in the proposed activities, and to offer them a wide array of experiences. Once again, however, it seems to be up to the teacher to decide what the children do in the classroom.

One participant also establishes a connection between participation and accessibility, stating that, because extra-curricular activities are not free of charge (families are required to pay an enrolment fee in order for their children to participate in such activities), not all children were allowed to participate.

In at least one of the contexts, the right to participation seems to be, in a way, a 'point of honour', given that the issue of children's rights is explicitly addressed inside the classroom. In another context, the relevance given to that issue is, in the participant's view, related to the school's current curriculum model, 'the HighScope [model], which places the child at the centre of everything' (excerpt from one of the narratives).

Participants were also asked to reflect upon their perceptions about the *school's role* in promoting children's rights. For many participants, the school has a fundamental role in the children's contact with their rights and duties: one participant states that 'the school should teach children about their rights' (excerpt from one of the narratives), while another one states that 'it is essential to promote that knowledge among children, who should grow up aware, not only of their duties, but also, and primarily, of their rights' (excerpt from one of the narratives). One other participant extends the school's responsibility in this area to include faculty members and non-teaching staff, while two other participants state that not only should the school be committed to implementing children's rights, the whole community should be made aware of their relevance.

In their analysis of this dimension, participants seem to be particularly critical of their practicum contexts: while a few note how, in the contexts they observed, the child is an active agent in their own learning process, others mention how they believe the schools should be more proactive in raising awareness about children's rights.

The school is identified, by several participants, as an exceptional context for the promotion of children's rights. For many, it should be a place where children are allowed to freely explore the world that surrounds them, to play, to participate freely and spontaneously, and also not to participate, if they so choose: 'children have the right to participation, but they also have the right to non-participation. They have the right to choose' (excerpt from one of the narratives).

Finally, in terms of the school's responsibility in the promotion of children's well-being, several participants mention how vital inter-institutional cooperation, and the engagement of the community in the school's life, can be. The stability of day-to-day interactions (between children, and between them and the adults), as well as the quality of the infrastructures and the diversity of stimuli, are also listed as contributing to the child's well-being at school. Several participants mention how children should be heard more, and given more opportunities for participation. Several others refer to a perceived need for more individualised attention to each child.

Closing Remarks: a future beyond austerity?

According to most of the participants' views, the ITE curriculum prepares them adequately in terms of the relevance of children's rights. However, this knowledge that they claim to hold appears to be mostly theoretical, as they seem, for the most part, unable to identify explicit instances where children's rights (namely, the right to participate in the school's daily life, and the decision-making processes lying therein) are respected or enforced.

The issue of children's well-being emerges, in many of the narratives, in connection with reports of how poverty is felt at school: participants state how children's lack of motivation for school may be connected with struggles at home, that children sometimes verbalise. In other cases, participants mention how some children did not bring the necessary supplies or a snack to school, were unable to afford extra-curricular activities (such as field trips), or sometimes started their school day without having a proper breakfast. When asked to reflect upon how practicum influenced their development as a (future) professional, several participants mention increased awareness towards issues such as child poverty, rationalisation of resources, and the fight for equity and social justice.

Finally, findings point to the need to reinforce the social and cultural dimension of ITE. Because there are no compulsory credits allocated to it, it is up to the higher education institutions to promote it, by integrating the ethical, social and cultural dimensions within other curricular components that have a required number of credits attached to them. ITE plays a key role in these demanding times, in Portugal, not only in providing student teachers with a more complex and broad picture of the teaching profession, but also in terms of a wider and more critical debate about education. The economic crisis and austerity measures have profoundly affected schools and teachers' lives, and, along with changes in policy and the curriculum of ITE in the post-Bologna context, have contributed to an accentuation of the academic and didactical perspectives, to the detriment of a more humanistic approach. As knowledge workers, teachers have a fundamental role in the social and cultural promotion of children and their families, and their training should prepare them accordingly.

While the future of ITE curricula is unpredictable, some recent changes in the Portuguese governmental and political landscape may have a significant impact on the country's socio-economic future, and therefore on children's rights. Following the 4 October 2015 election, the most-voted-for party coalition failed to secure majority parliamentary support and therefore had its government programme rejected. On 24 November, and following the Socialist Party's negotiations (and agreement) with the Left Bloc (BE), the Portuguese Communist Party (PCP) and the Ecologist Party 'The Greens' (PEV), a new prime minister was appointed; the cabinet members of the 21st Constitutional Government of Portugal took their oath of office two days later. Among the number of measures approved in the following weeks, the so-called Income Package (*Pacote Rendimento*) seems particularly noteworthy in terms of families' well-being – and, therefore, that of children – in that it establishes the restitution of pensions and social supplements (with a budget of about 50 million euros for the unconditional basic income), and an increase in family allowances (namely, for single-parent families, of around 15%). The extinction of the surcharge over the income tax (corresponding to 3.5% of taxable income that exceeds the national minimum wage), in force since 2013, has also been discussed: the government's proposal is for this surcharge to drop to 1.75% in 2016 and be eliminated in 2017. The extinction of income reductions in public administration, and of the extraordinary solidarity contribution (a tax levied on the monthly value earned by pensioners/retirees) has also had majority approval. There has been at least one legislative action that directly pertains to children's rights (namely, Article 8 of the UNCRC), ensuring equal rights of access to adoption and civil sponsorship for same-sex couples.

While it is impossible to assess, at this point, the true impact such measures (and others) will have on the country's socio-economic situation, there seems to be a general sense of expectation and a renewed attention to social issues, from which children may benefit particularly.

Notes

[1] '*Estado Novo*' (which directly translates as 'New State') was the official name of the authoritarian, autocratic and corporatist regime in force in Portugal for a period of 41 years, between the approval of the 1933 Constitution up until its overthrow by the 25 April 1974 Revolution.

[2] '*Lei de Bases de Organização da Previdência*', known as Law no. 1884, published on 16 March 1935.

[3] After Marcello Caetano replaced António de Oliveira Salazar as prime minister of the '*Estado Novo*' regime.

[4] The 'PARES' programme, that supported the construction of new childcare facilities, was implemented during this period.

[5] Food Emergency Programme.

[6] In its present form, the UNCRC consists of 54 articles pertaining to child-specific needs and rights, including the right to life, to a name and an identity, to be raised within a family or cultural grouping, and to participate fully in family, cultural and social life.

[7] Articles 12-15 of the UNCRC generally acknowledge children's ability to form their own views, as well as the right to express them freely, to be heard and to have their views acted on when appropriate (freedom of speech, freedom of thought and freedom of association). Article 12, specifically, clearly states that the views of children should be taken into consideration in matters directly pertaining to them – that is, that children are to be seen as experts in their own issues (United Nations, 1989).

[8] 'On this issue, I believe I know about the historical evolution of its existence and its implications on the views of childhood' (excerpt from one of the narratives).

References

Benavente, A., Aníbal, G., Martins, J. et al (2014) *O Estado da Educação num Estado Intervencionado. Portugal 2014* [The State of Education in an Interventioned State. Portugal 2014]. Lisbon: Op.Edu.

Cardoso, J.L. & Rocha, M.M. (2003) Corporativismo e Estado Providência (1933-1962) [Corporatism and Welfare State (1933-1962)], *Ler História*, 45, 111-135.

Chzhen, Y. (2014) Subjective Impact of the Economic Crisis on Households with Children in 17 European Countries. Innocenti Working Paper No. 2014-09. Florence: UNICEF Office of Research.

Clandinin, D.J., Pushor, D. & Orr, A.M. (2007) Navigating Sites for Narrative Inquiry, *Journal of Teacher Education*, 58(1), 21-35. http://dx.doi.org/10.1177/0022487106296218

Danner, S. & Jonyniene, Z. (2012) Participation of Children in Democratic Decision-making in Kindergarten: experiences in Germany and Lithuania, *Socialinis Darbas/Social Work*, 11(2), 411-420.

EAPN (2014) *Indicadores sobre a pobreza. Dados Europeus e Nacionais* [Indicators about poverty. European and national data]. Porto: Rede Europeia Anti-Pobreza/Portugal.

Ek, A., Ideland, M., Jönsson, S. & Malmberg, C. (2013) The Tension between Marketisation and Academisation in Higher Education, *Studies in Higher Education*, 9, 1305-1318. http://dx.doi.org/10.1080/03075079.2011.619656

Elliott, J. (2005) *Using Narrative in Social Research: qualitative and quantitative approaches*. London: SAGE.

Estanque, E. (2012) O Estado Social em Causa: Instituições, políticas sociais e movimentos sociolaborais no contexto europeu [The Social State at Stake: institutions, social policies and socio-labor movements in the European context], *Finisterra – Revista de Reflexão e Crítica*, 73, 39-80.

European Commission (2013) Commission Recommendation of 20.2.2013, Investing in Children: breaking the cycle of disadvantage. http://eur-lex.europa.eu/legal-content/EN/TXT/PDF/?uri=CELEX:32013H0112&from=EN (accessed 30 October 2015).

Eurostat (2013a) General Government Gross Debt. http://epp.eurostat.ec.europa.eu/tgm/table.do?tab=table&plugin=1&language=en&pcode=tsdde410 (accessed 6 August 2013).

Eurostat (2013b) Government Deficit/surplus, Debt and Associated Data. http://appsso.eurostat.ec.europa.eu/nui/show.do (accessed 6 August 2013).

Glaser, B.G. & Strauss, A.L. (1967) *The Discovery of Grounded Theory: strategies for qualitative research*. Chicago: Aldine.

Grilo, M.M. (Coord.) (2013) *As Crianças e a Crise em Portugal. Vozes de Crianças, Políticas Públicas e Indicadores Sociais* [Children and the Crisis in Portugal. Voices of Children, Public Policies and Social Indicators]. Lisbon: UNICEF Portuguese Committee.

Hollway, W. & Jefferson, T. (2000) *Doing Qualitative Research Differently: free association, narrative and the interview method*. London: SAGE.

International Monetary Fund (2009) *World Economic Outlook: a survey by the staff of the International Monetary Fund*. Washington, DC: International Monetary Fund.

Leahy, A., Healy, S. & Murphy, M. (2014) The European Crisis and its Human Cost: a call for fair alternatives and solutions. Crisis Monitoring Report 2014. s.l.: Caritas Europa.

Lúcio, J. & I'Anson, J. (2015) Children as Members of a Community: citizenship, participation and educational development – an introduction to the special issue, *European Educational Research Journal*, 14(2), 129-137. http://dx.doi.org/10.1177/1474904115571794

Martorano, B. (2014) The Consequences of the Recent Economic Crisis and Government Reactions for Children. Innocenti Working Paper No. 2014-05. Florence: UNICEF Office of Research.

Miles, M.B. & Huberman, A.M. (1994) *Qualitative Data Analysis*. Thousand Oaks, CA: SAGE.

National Bureau of Economic Research (2010) US Business Cycle Expansions and Contractions. http://www.nber.org/cycles/cyclesmain.html (accessed 2 November 2015).

Pereirinha, J.A. & Carolo, D.F. (2009) *A Construção do Estado-Providência em Portugal. Evolução da despesa social de 1935 a 2003. Documento de trabalho n. 36* [The Construction of the Welfare State in Portugal. Evolution of Social Expenditure from 1935 to 2003. Working paper no. 36]. Lisbon: Gabinete de História Económica e Social.

Ramos, M.C.P. (2011) Economia Solidária, Plural e Ética, na Promoção do Emprego, da Cidadania e da Coesão Social [Solidarity, Plural and Ethical Economy, in the Promotion of Employment, Citizenship and Social Cohesion], *Laboreal*, 7(1), 81-84.

UNICEF Office of Research (2014) Children of the Recession: the impact of the economic crisis on child well-being in rich countries. Innocenti Report Card 12. Florence: UNICEF Office of Research.

United Nations (1989) United Nations Convention on the Rights of the Child. http://www.ohchr.org/Documents/ProfessionalInterest/crc.pdf (accessed 5 December 2014).

United Nations (2014) Concluding Observations on the Third and Fourth Periodic Reports of Portugal. http://tbinternet.ohchr.org/_layouts/treatybodyexternal/Download.aspx?symbolno=Crc/C/Prt/Co/3-4&Lang=En (accessed 31 October 2015).

CHAPTER 6

Rights without a Remedy? Children's Privacy, Social Governance and the UNCRC

GORDON TAIT & MALLIHAI TAMBYAH

SUMMARY Article 16 of the UNCRC states that children have the right to privacy; but what does this actually mean? The notions of rights, privacy and childhood are all socially and historically contingent. Consequently, framing children's privacy as a natural right could be seen as problematic, to say the least. Pressures within the family towards increased surveillance of children, as well as educational imperatives for greater record keeping, increased use of personal data, closer scrutiny of student/staff interactions, and concerns over student conduct and public liability have all reduced children's privacy rather than augmented it. As such, given that children's right to privacy appears to be 'a right without a remedy', does this mean that Article 16 is ultimately pointless? Far from it. As with many elements of the UNCRC, it sets out an important symbolic benchmark for framing debates. Irrespective of the conceptual and legal shortcomings of 'children's privacy', Article 16 puts the issue squarely on the table, and forces other social and governmental imperatives, rationalities and mandates to factor it into their calculations.

Introduction: Article 16 of the UNCRC

It is tempting to position the United Nations Convention of the Rights of the Child (UNCRC) (United Nations, 1989) as the final step in the long path towards the full recognition of our collective responsibilities for the young. After all, with 193 signatories, it is the most ratified of all human rights treaties. Australia ratified the convention in 1990 and it builds upon a range of other international instruments, such as the Geneva Declaration (League of Nations, 1924), the Universal Declaration on Human Rights (United Nations, 1948), and the Declaration on the Rights of the Child (United Nations, 1959). These agreements were themselves built upon a wave of domestic legislation that occurred in most western industrial countries throughout the nineteenth century – for example, the Australian state of Victoria's Neglected and Criminal Children's Act (Government of Victoria, Australia, 1864; Bessant & Watts, 2008).

However, true social and legal progress rarely follows policy initiatives, and unfortunately the ratification of the UNCRC has not immediately transformed Australia into an ideal state vis-à-vis the rights of children. As with all other signatories to the convention, positive changes in the lives of children have often been slow in coming, fractional in their deployment, and subject to reversal if left unchecked. Arguably, there are three reasons for this. The first reason is governmental. Just because there exists the intent to achieve a particular governmental outcome, whether by means of specific laws, conventions, policies, programs or interventions, it does not mean that outcome is guaranteed, or even that it is particularly likely. Unsurprisingly, there continue to be neglected and criminal children in the state of Victoria, even after the 1864 legislation, in spite of the best intentions of the state parliament. As Wickham (1993) notes, governance is necessarily a continually failing operation and it is only through an ongoing dissatisfaction with that governance that new programs are organised and implemented, and new sites of intervention delineated. The very nature of governmental programs, including international conventions, makes them ambiguous, partial and inexact, resulting in the targets of government 'refusing to respond according to the programmatic logic that seeks to govern them' (Rose & Miller 1992, p. 190).

The second reason is legal. There is certainly an overwhelming consensus of opinion at an international level that children's rights are worthy of demarcation and protection; the United States and Somalia remain the only two nations yet to sign the UNCRC. However, signing an instrument such as this does not immediately make the contents of that instrument part of a country's domestic law. That is, Australia, for example, can join the global community and signal its general agreement with the overall tenor of the convention by adding its signature to the list and then do nothing in terms of actually altering Australian domestic legislation to meet the new standards. As Tobin (2008, p. 24) notes:

> Australia has remained obdurate in its refusal to implement the CRC. This is not to say that children do not have human rights in Australia ... however, there has been no deliberate or concerted effort to use the CRC and the notion of children as rights bearers as a benchmark against which to develop, implement and monitor laws and policies affecting children.

This is not an unusual occurrence. Australia has ratified all seven United Nations human rights conventions and is yet to give the force of domestic law to any of them. With particular regard to the UNCRC, there exist ongoing differences between the articles of the UNCRC and Australian domestic law. This disparity occurs principally within areas such as the incarceration of the young, the over-representation of Aboriginal and Torres Strait Islander children in the criminal justice system, the placing of children in care, and the disaggregation of data concerning ethnic, refugee, migrant and internally displaced children, as relating to abuse, neglect and sexual exploitation (Mitchell, 2014).

The third reason is definitional. The UNCRC is comprised of 54 articles, largely covering the provision of particular sets of rights, the protection of children from specific types of conduct and outcome, and the guarantee of participation in society within defined civil and political rights (Lansdown, 1994). However, the subject matter of these articles is not always immediately self-evident, and even where it is, its actual intention may be subject to debate. For example, Article 12 concerns the right of children to have their views taken into account. The question here is what does this actually mean? Taken into account by whom, to what extent, and in what contexts? These questions, as they relate to Article 12 alone, have been the subject of considerable discussion (Fernando, 2013).

The same definitional issue arises in the case for Article 16, the central focus of this chapter. This article provides a right to privacy for children, as follows:

> *Article 16*
> 1. No child shall be subjected to arbitrary or unlawful interference with his or her privacy, family, or correspondence, nor to unlawful attacks on his or her honour and reputation.
> 2. The child has the right to the protection of the law against such interference or attacks. (United Nations, 1989)

This is undoubtedly a laudable sentiment, but privacy is a complex and elusive concept to define for adults, let alone children. So what is the right to privacy and can children possess this right? Moreover, does the provision of this right by the UNCRC actually mean anything in practice in Australia, both in general, and more specifically, within the field of education? These questions provide the focus for the remainder of this chapter.

Rights and Childhood

Before unpacking the complexities of a child's right to privacy under the UNCRC, it is first appropriate to address the issue of rights in a more general sense. After all, what exactly are rights, and to what extent can we say that children have them? There are a number of approaches to this issue, but the one taken by international instruments such as the UNCRC is that of *natural rights*. Most frequently associated with the seventeenth-century English philosopher John Locke, this approach asserts that while some rights, often called conventional rights, are allocated on the basis of particular social, legal or political systems, other rights are anterior to this. These other, more fundamental rights are not given by society, and neither can they be taken away by it. Such natural rights are regarded as 'somehow part of the fabric of nature itself' (Tannsjo, 2002, p. 76), and certainly part of what it is to be human. Probably the most famous of these natural rights are the rights to 'life, liberty and the pursuit of happiness' (Locke, 1689).

The right to privacy, as set out in Article 16 of the UNCRC, is similarly positioned as a natural right. That is, this right is possessed by all of us simply by virtue of our existence as self-determining moral subjects. While specific legal systems or cultural practices around the globe (those conferring conventional rights) may seek to place limitations on individual privacy, or even deny it altogether, the assertion here is that there exists an a-priori natural right to privacy that cannot be legitimately overridden irrespective of context. The question now arises: to what extent can children have rights, including the right to privacy? As previously discussed, though this may now seem like a rather unnecessary question, this has by no means always been the case. In western thinking, children only began to be allocated legal rights from the mid-nineteenth century onwards. Certainly, under Roman law, with the doctrine of *patria potestas*, a father had the right of life and death over his children (Borkowski, 1994). Those children had no rights of their own in any contemporary sense.

Thomas (2011) suggests that the move to grant natural rights to children can best be understood as existing between two poles, the first seeking to protect children from exploitation and abuse, the other seeking to liberate children from their position as 'lesser' humans, thus according them the privileges and self-determination available to adults. Arguably it is the 'protector' approach that characterised the first wave of legislation granting rights to children, principally including the right not to be exploited at work, and the right not to be neglected by parents. However, since the 1960s the focus has fallen upon giving children the right to a greater say in their own affairs. This 'liberator' approach has sought to challenge the limits placed upon children's right, limits often subliminally founded in the Roman tradition that, in the final analysis, still positions children as parental property (Farson, 1974; Holt, 1975). Thomas (2011, p. 5) goes on to suggest a middle path between these two approaches, one which:

> should reflect children's developing competence, offering
> them protection as long as they need it combined with
> empowerment as soon as they are ready for it, with restrictions

on their freedom and autonomy only where these can be
justified in terms of maximising their future choices.

This seems to be exactly the approach adopted by the UNCRC. The
convention is divided into a number of parts. While the entire document
has 54 articles, the substantive component of the convention is dealt
with within part 1, which covers the first 41 articles. These articles cover
a range of rights, the majority of which can be understood in terms of
either the right to survival and security (i.e. protection rights) or the right
to social participation (i.e. liberation rights) (specifically Articles 12-17).
Article 16, conferring upon children the right to privacy, is one of these
liberation rights.

In spite of the overwhelming number of countries that have ratified
the UNCRC, it should be pointed out that the question of whether
children should have rights at all is far from a settled one. Some
commentators assert that 'rights' are an inappropriate mechanism to
insert within the organisational fabric of the family (Schoeman, 1980).
They contend that the family is a unique form of human association, one
ostensibly based upon love, trust and mutual respect, and to introduce
clumsy legal obligations, such as rights, into this setting risks causing
irreparable damage to our most fundamental of institutions. Indeed, the
counterposing issue of 'parents' rights' is one of the main reasons the
USA has refused to ratify the convention. A second critique of allocating
rights to children is the claim that they lack the capacity to make
informed choices, upon which the exercise of rights is based. Schapiro
(2003) suggests that children lack the intellectual proficiency to make the
choices necessary to protect and advance their own interests. Taking this
argument even further, she proposes that children are incapable of
making their own choices, whether good or bad, as they do not yet exist
in the state of full self-governing personhood that separates them, in a
Kantian sense, from a state of nature. That is, there has not yet developed
a complete, autonomous subject to whom the choice can be legitimately
allocated.

The UNCRC answers the question of whether children have the
competence to be allocated rights by adopting an 'evolving capacities'
approach. Article 5 of the UNCRC states that an appropriate balance
between the protection and liberation of children should be struck 'in a
manner consistent with the evolving capacities of the child'. To put it
another way, the convention recognises that while the family is the
central guiding institution for children, it is also the case that they will
become more independent as their capacities develop. Lansdown (2005)
notes that this principle has significant implications for the human rights
of the child. That is, rather than simply adopting the old, universalising
'ages and stages' approach to child development, the convention
recognises that given the range of experiences and environments faced by
children around the globe, such children will 'evolve capacities' at

different rates, and therefore the requirement both for protection and for a greater say in their own affairs will also be subject to significant variation.

The Past: the evolution of the right to privacy

Having decided upon this approach, how does this then relate to the notion of privacy and the contention that children have a right to it? After all, when it comes to privacy, just what are we referring to here? Solove (2008, p. 45) contends that attempts to find a satisfactory, singular definition of privacy are doomed to failure, as privacy is rather 'an umbrella term that refers to a wide and disparate group of related things'. While undeniably far from perfect, one of the longest-standing and most-quoted formulations of the right to privacy has been 'the right to be left alone' (Warren & Brandeis, 1890).

Under Australian law, there are two central types of privacy: the first is the most straightforward, and involves personal information privacy, which is afforded some protection in the Privacy Act 1988 (Cth) (Commonwealth Government of Australia, 1988). However, the second type of privacy is a more general right to personal privacy, and this is not protected within Australia, either by legislation or by the common law. There is some protection, in a very piecemeal way, within defamation and trespass law, but nothing that coheres into what might be described as a 'legal right to privacy'. There has been legal discussion for fifteen years regarding the introduction of a tort of invasions of privacy, but this has yet to produce any results. (There is also a lack of a legal remedy for invasion of personal privacy in the USA, where some limited protection can be inferred through the Fourth Amendment, and likewise in the UK, where at most some equally limited rights can be found in the Human Rights Act 1998). Simply put, there is no single, unequivocal 'right to privacy' in Australia. This is perhaps surprising as the desire for privacy is often depicted as one of the most fundamental of all human needs, so it would be logical to think that our legal system would have sought to protect it.

In her text on legal conceptions of privacy in the twenty-first century, Rengel (2013) begins by restating this foundational, essentialist understanding of privacy. The logic here is that such a notion of privacy readily lends itself to its depiction as an a-priori natural right, with all the legal consequences of that assessment, including the belief that it deserves to be protected within instruments such as the UNCRC.

> The concept of privacy is one that is difficult to define but at the same time has a basic and intuitive feel to it ... some have argued that the right to privacy exists prior and independent to any political society and prior to any system of law. That argument leads to the theory that the right to privacy is

grounded in humans' intrinsic and natural needs, and is
necessary for the orderly functioning of society. (Rengel, 2013,
p. 9)

Arguably, there are two problems with this domain assumption. First, it can readily be argued that this approach is culturally contingent. That is, the concept of privacy as proposed here applies to a very western way of thinking, behaving and 'being', and draws on the history of the West where the individual is prized and where the small or nuclear family has become the norm. This may not be the case in Aboriginal, Eastern or South Asian communities, or indeed anywhere where the western paradigm is not the norm, with different family structures and strong extended family and community relationships. In other words, there will be communities in Australia where these western notions of privacy are not as strong, depending on how well people have assimilated western ways of thinking and living.

Second, this understanding of the need for privacy as an essential human requirement is not supported by historians, even when solely considering western societies. Indeed, the best evidence suggests that the desire for 'privacy' is better positioned as a historically contingent and flexible expectation that only began to emerge in the late medieval period. So fundamental are issues of 'privacy' to our modern sense of self, it is difficult to imagine a time when they would not have existed. However, even well into medieval times in Europe, all basic life functions were unashamedly conducted in public. After all, at this time there was no reason, or opportunity, for it to have been otherwise, and to say this would be problematic for most of us now would be something of an understatement.

Interestingly, this change in sensibilities came about largely as a result of two mundane domestic inventions: the internal chimney and the corridor. The logic here is that towards the end of the thirteenth century, there began in Europe what has been referred to as the 'Little Ice Age'. According to Burke (1978), the steep fall in temperatures meant that it was no longer physically viable for everyone to huddle around a single fire for warmth – one always sat below a large (heat-squandering) hole in the roof, the only smoke-removal technology available. The invention of the internal chimney allowed for the safer and more efficient use of fire within the home; smoke could now be easily removed, and heat retained. This had the secondary effect of permitting a number of different fires within the same house, as well as using the previous smoke-filled space in the top of the house for an upstairs area, and consequently smaller rooms began to proliferate (Dresbeck, 1971). It consequently became possible to think of certain domestic spaces as belonging to particular individuals, and it was from this starting point that the concept of privacy could begin to emerge, with all the associated implications for human behaviour.

The second closely associated technological change involves the invention of the corridor. Though not widely socially distributed until the eighteenth century (Jarzombek, 2010), the appearance of corridors in stately homes meant that it was no longer necessary to walk through other people's bedrooms to get to your own, an action that had previously been an inconvenience rather than an invasion of a private space. By the process of prestigious emulation, ordinary people soon had corridors and for the first time people had rooms of their own that no one else had reason to enter. So whereas wanting to be alone was once viewed with suspicion (what could he/she possibly be *doing* in there?), all the necessary elements were now in place for the newfound 'desire for privacy' to morph into 'an instinctive, innate human attribute' (Spacks, 2003).

To restate: in no way were these two inventions ever designed with the development of 'privacy' in mind, per se; they simply played a pivotal role in allowing the concept to emerge. That is, just as Postman (1994) argued that the printing press had the unforeseen side effect of eventually allowing the development of a whole new category of human – the child – so too the chimney and the corridor had their own unrelated side effects. One combined outcome of all these mundane technological changes, five hundred years later, is that it becomes possible to assert that 'children' have a natural right to 'privacy'. Of course, just because it turns out that constructs like 'children' and 'privacy' are not really natural entities, this does not mean that they still do not occupy privileged positions within our social and legal fabric, positions deserving of the full protection of the law, both domestic and international.

Having established a foundation for addressing the issues of both rights and privacy, it is now possible to examine some of the ways in which children's 'right to privacy' is addressed and managed within the Australian context. After all, if we have reached a global consensus that children's rights are worth protecting, in particular their right to privacy as set out in Article 16 of the UNCRC, then surely there ought to be some evidence of this within the social body. The next part of this chapter will focus upon two domains in which debates about childhood privacy are usually played out: that is, the home and the school. Within these sites, it will now be suggested that the notion of childhood privacy is becoming defined by its relationship to various mechanisms of social governance.

The Present: childhood as a regulated space

Following the work of Foucault (1977, 2001), it is most frequently argued that contemporary forms of governance largely operate through regulating the conduct of the population. This regulation occurs in a variety of ways, and not necessarily according to any single logic; however, it has unquestionably been shaped by the historical forces of liberalism, a philosophy of rule that emerged in the late seventeenth century. Liberalism, as a series of debates about the extent of the power of the State, contended that it was acceptable for the State to be involved in issues such as law enforcement and international affairs, but it should stay out of the running of the economic marketplace and, crucially, out of the 'private' domain of the family and the raising of children.

In spite of this final element of boundary-setting, it soon became apparent that the production of the next generation of citizens was far too important to be left to chance, or to the whims and vagaries of individual families. Consequently, the State began to involve itself in the process at arm's length, steering the direction of child-raising, while seeming not to do so. This 'government at a distance' involved two main sites of subtle intervention: the family and the school. As a consequence of this form of governance, childhood quickly became an intensely regulated space; as Rose (1990, p. 123) notes:

> Childhood is the most intensely governed sector of human existence. In different ways, and different times, and by many different routes varying from one sector of society to another, the health, welfare and destiny of children has been linked in thoughts and practice to the destiny of the nation and the responsibilities of the state.

Whether governing directly, or indirectly through relays such as the family and the school, the central strategy has always been to amass as much statistical data as possible, through which it then becomes possible to differentiate and then normalise the population, producing suitably docile and manageable citizens. Each individuated citizen is constituted through the keeping of increasingly vast amounts of data; the data relate to matters of health, education, criminal conduct, economics, welfare, sexuality, consumption and parenting, to name but a few.

Importantly, these data are collected in often disparate and piecemeal ways through ongoing social surveillance. While the great institutions of modernity – the school, the prison, the hospital, the factory – have all been structured around the continual surveillatory power of the panopticon, surveillance also takes on a much more nebulous form. The family may have been regarded, and may have regarded itself, as an essentially private space; however, in practice, governmental assessments of its internal workings, its combined capacities and its economic trajectory are the very material by which society is so effectively regulated.

This apparent paradox forms the central problematic of this chapter. Documents such as the UNCRC mandate the 'natural' right of children to privacy, yet the central model of governance for modern bureaucratic societies is to closely surveil their populations to acquire the information necessary for effective management. Perhaps a closer assessment of the current parameters of privacy concerning the family and the school will help clarify this issue. That is, to what extent can children expect privacy in these two sites?

Children, Privacy and the Home

The family is no longer simply a group of related individuals, sharing mutual affection and a common name, as it might once have been. Donzelot (1979) suggests that the modern 'pedagogic' family is a very specific creation, in that it has become a central component of contemporary governance. This new type of family was to be regulated by a range of medical, educational and psychological experts, and these experts linked the inner workings of the family unit to the broadest objective of government. By what Donzelot (1979, p. 169) refers to as 'the subtle regulation of images', it becomes possible to construct desirable and effective norms of family life, and these images recruited mothers into becoming 'good' mothers, a necessary prerequisite for the parallel production of 'good' children. The important issue here is that 'good' parents provide protection and support for their children across every conceivable physical, emotional and economic eventuality. Such parents are also aware of the risks faced by children in the twenty-first century and surveil their children accordingly. Indeed, within the contemporary pedagogic family, parents who do not accept the help and guidance of external experts in raising their children are now deemed to be bad parents; parents who do not closely surveil their children's activities, particularly online, are now deemed to be negligent parents.

So if privacy is understood as 'the right to be left alone', this now appears to run counter to many notions of good parenting. Shmueli and Blecher-Prigat (2011, p. 768) note that, in some ways, children are caught between their needs *as* children and the exercise of their rights, such as that set out in Article 16 of the UNCRC:

> Children are inherently dependent upon and connected to others ... in most cases, they should not and must not be 'let alone'. Indeed if this is the only way to understand the right to privacy, then recognising children's right to privacy would surely be to be seen as 'abandoning' them to their rights.

Adding further confusion as to how to conceptualise the notion of privacy, the evidence suggests that modern children are not as bothered about their privacy as their parents are. Indeed, the central focus of children's concerns over privacy *is* their parents (Marwick et al, 2010). It turns out that the desire for a space of their own, away from the constant gaze of their parents, and the desire to communicate freely, whether online or off, without the filter of parental supervision, constitutes the main 'privacy' issues for children. Of course, from the perspective of the good parent these concerns need to be placed within the wider 'risk' context of Internet predators, teenage drug use, radicalisation, domestic accident, or any number of other perceived dangers, real or otherwise, that delimit their children's right to privacy.

One of the central problems when addressing the issue of children's privacy is the assumption that the most important intrusions on that privacy will have their origins outside the family. The notion of evolving capacities presumes that the family can protect the interests of the children until the children can take responsibility for themselves. However, if the central issue is actually intra-familial privacy, then it may well be that the overall logic of the UNCRC is not well suited to this particular right. After all, the interests of the child risk becoming subsumed within those of the family, given that there is no necessary unity between these interests. Within the home, then, the 'privacy problem' primarily involves tensions between family privacy and the privacy of individual family members, particularly children. Currently, the children of 'good' parents are often highly surveilled, and ongoing moral panics, particularly about online dangers, are tipping the balance in the protection vs. liberation equation. As will now be discussed, these concerns are also played out within the school.

Children, Privacy and the School

In schools, there is only a limited promise or expectation of student privacy. As previously mentioned, contemporary educational institutions are based around continual surveillance and this panoptic design mitigates against the existence of sites where students can readily avoid the gaze of teachers. However, contemporary education research continues to show that some of the more recent changes within the fabric of western schooling systems are particularly significant to the issue of privacy as they speak to the augmentation of existing disciplinary strategies, as well as to the impact of different, often contradictory, social and ethical rationalities.

1. Surveilling the Student Population

Whereas early iterations of school surveillance involved a relatively simple gallery/monitorial organisational system along with some basic academic record keeping, this has evolved into a complex web of governmental intelligibility targeting the child (Tait, 2000). Every conceivable element of the child's capacities is to be measured and normalised; no aspects of the child are to remain hidden or private. As Rose (1990) concludes, the very soul of the child is to be rendered amenable to governance. Likewise, the possibilities of direct physical surveillance have also increased. It is no longer sufficient to deploy panoptic architecture across the school – this has now been augmented by the increasing use of CCTV cameras, which are 'routinely' being used in classrooms, particularly in the United Kingdom, with over 90% of secondary schools now using them (Paton, 2014). This raises complex questions of privacy, not only for children, but also for teaching staff. After all, who has access to the recordings, and for what purpose?

2. Education and the Rise of Big Data

We now live in the era of Big Data. Since the mid-nineteenth century, modern governance has been built upon what Hacking (1982) referred to as an 'avalanche of printed numbers', which has allowed the construction of ever-increasing categories of difference within the population. However, the recently developed ability to correlate instantly almost unfathomably huge amounts of data means that the possibilities of comparison, differentiation and intervention are now almost limitless. This has a number of important implications for the relationship between schools, children and their privacy.

First, given the oceans of data that are now being generated within our education systems, and given that these data are both permanent and instantly accessible, the risk is now that every single element, incident and disappointment within an entire schooling career can be accessed and scrutinised by a future employer, a university admissions officer or the police. This hardly seems to be a fair and appropriate use of what may otherwise be a long-forgotten, personal and private schooling history. If privacy is the right to be left alone, does this extend to leaving data relating to their educational pasts alone? Second, the governmental intelligibility made possible through Big Data does not stop at the gates to the school. As yet, there are no widely accepted protocols in place to determine who may and may not utilise those data, or indeed, who even owns those data. The data are often not only sold to educational companies producing learning packages or preparation materials for standardised testing, they are sometimes even accessible to business in general. The issue here is whether the right to privacy for children extends to the right for companies not to make a profit off their data without their express consent. Finally, probably the most pressing issue regarding Big Data and privacy concerns national meta-data surveillance, an issue which affects not only children, but every single one of us. Governments now have the ability to record and analyse all electronic communications – phone calls, texts, emails, Internet searches – all in the name of national security. These communications are then subject to meta-analysis, where not only patterns of behaviour and association are delineated, but also particular 'persons of interest' can be isolated and tracked. As Stockman (2013) states:

> So the issue is not really how to protect privacy in the age of Big Data. Privacy, in the old fashioned sense, is already gone. The question now is: How can we be sure that the Big Data out there will be used only for good?

Arguably the close surveillance of children in schools – with all the associated implications for children's privacy – is also motivated by reasons other than ongoing mundane social governance. The evidence would suggest that two other factors also play into this equation: concerns over the sexualisation of children, and concerns related to public liability for injury and abuse.

3. Schools and the Moral Panic over the Sexualisation of Children

There are several factors which, in combination, have resulted in increased concerns over the sexuality of children within the schooling environment, with all the concomitant consequences for children's privacy (Tait, 2001). First, following Postman (1994), children are no longer as protected from knowledge about sexual issues as was once the case, and this has resulted not only in the shrinking of the category of 'child' in a general sense, but also in the sexualising of individuals who were once deemed far too young. This has resulted in a deep sense of disquiet as society tries to come to terms with this new reality.

Second, and largely as a result of this, there is now a continuing worry about the vulnerability of children to sexual predation. Within the framework of evolving capacities, there is again an unresolved tension between the need to protect children and the perceived right, largely coming from the children themselves, that they should be allowed to make their own choices – which should not come as a surprise, given the cultural sexualisation to which they are exposed on a daily basis. As a result, children are taught about stranger danger, 'how to be safe' and age-appropriate sex education in primary school. One policy outcome of this fear of sexual predation is the belief that children need to be surveilled constantly and the school needs to be a sealed environment to protect from predatory outsiders. Once again, this has implications for children's rights to privacy.

Another associated outcome is a climate of fear and suspicion vis-à-vis male teachers. Male teachers are now being forced to teach differently, not for pedagogic reasons, but simply to avoid the risk of suspicion or false accusation. Most schools now have 'no touch' policies, for both male and female teachers. These policies are deemed to go some way towards protecting children/potential victims – along with open-door policies, never-be-alone-with-**A**-student policies, record-every-contact policies, and so on – all of which mitigate against the possibility of privacy for children within the school.

4. Education and Public Liability

A central component of the contemporary legal landscape is the issue of public liability. Like all public institutions, businesses, sporting organisations and workplaces, schools also need to be concerned about their exposure to civil actions in cases of negligence and personal injury. This has resulted in a workplace environment where all conceivable risks need to be recognised, assessed and minimised. Teachers and administrators evaluate all elements of the schooling environment, both for the safety of their students, but also to minimise their legal liability if anything goes wrong. This extends far beyond the perceived risk of sexual abuse, and mostly focuses on the risk of injury, whether from negligence, badly planned teaching and learning activities, contact sport, lack of supervision or the conduct of other students. Schools may limit the scope of educational activities outside school, for example, school excursions, service learning/volunteer activities or even competitive sport conducted in public facilities.

The important issue here is that zones of pupil privacy equate directly to zones of economic and personal risk. The unfortunate legal truth is that a teacher who does not closely and constantly surveil their pupils is a negligent teacher. Much as a teacher may think that pupils are entitled to some degree of privacy within the school, their professional responsibilities are more likely to push them towards taking a more cautious, risk-averse approach to the matter. Ultimately, a nebulous, somewhat ill-defined 'right to student privacy' is no match for a formal, clearly defined legal responsibility for student well-being.

In summary, childhood is an intensely regulated time and two of the principal sites for this regulation are the home and the school. Despite good intentions, in many ways the information required to govern children effectively in these locations means that their privacy is very much a secondary concern. Contemporary research into both the home and the school has shown that children may well have 'a right to privacy' but they are also subject to an array of governmental interventions and forms of scrutiny that mitigate against that right.

The Future: is Article 16 of the UNCRC of any value?

From the ground covered so far in this chapter, there seem to be three main constraints operating in relation to the implementation of any right to children's privacy. First, as has just been discussed, childhood is a heavily regulated domain. A crucial part of that regulation involves the amassing of sufficient information by which to differentiate chosen populations effectively. 'The right to privacy' and 'needs of government' often work in opposition to each other, and if the Edward Snowden affair tells us anything, it is that the 'needs of government' will ultimately triumph over granting children the right to privacy, a decision which is always going to be understood through the conceptual prism of 'evolving capacities'.

Second, the notion of privacy itself is a complex one, and far from being an 'essential human right and requirement', it appears instead to be an evolving historical construct. The common definition of 'the right to be left alone' constitutes a rather nebulous starting point even for general discussions about the parameters of privacy, never mind when considering the linguistic specificity required of black letter law – domestic or international. Certainly, the notion of privacy is not clarified within the UNCRC. This is compounded by the observation that 'privacy' is something of a plural, umbrella concept. More accurately, it is most likely best understood as located within a series of Wittgensteinian family resemblances, which refers to an understanding of language founded upon connecting particular uses of the same word. That is, rather than seeking a single essence that defines the meaning of a word such as 'privacy', the meaning is shaped instead within a set of overlapping similarities, with no necessity that any one similarity is common to all; it is a series of threads that together make up a single string (Wittgenstein, 1952).

Finally, in addition to these fundamental problems of definition and conceptualisation, there appears to be little prescribed legal support for a 'right to privacy' within Australia. As previously mentioned, there is no general right to privacy under Australian law. While there is some legal protection for personal information, and scattered coverage under civil trespass and defamation laws, this does not cohere into anything formal, coherent or comprehensive – a situation shared by most other western legal systems.

No Rights without a Remedy?

Given all the qualifications on the very possibility of a child's right to privacy, what then does the UNCRC Article 16 actually represent? In truth, seemingly nothing particularly concrete, and certainly nothing backed by solid legal remedies. If there are only scattered remedies for various breaches of different types of privacy under Australian domestic law, then an imprecise international convention like the UNCRC is unlikely to speak to any effective remedies of enforcement at all. And if there are no remedies attached to breach, then what is the point of having the right in the first place?

This logic forms the basis for one of the most well-known of all legal aphorisms: 'No rights without a remedy', which can arguably be applied to all legal systems, and certainly to the issue of privacy within the UNCRC. The claim here is that the law protects you only insofar as you have a remedy for its breach, an assertion which has its origins in the most famous of all American Supreme Court cases, *Maybury vs. Madison* (1802), which set out the principle of judicial review. In that case, Chief Justice Marshall stated: 'The very essence of civil liberty consists in the right of every individual to claim the protection of the laws ... The government of the United States has been emphatically termed a government of laws, and not of men. It will certainly cease to deserve this high appellation, if the laws furnish no remedy for the violation of a vested right.' If Article 16 sets out a child's right to privacy, but offers no suggestions as to a remedy for breach of this right – whether that is because of the confusing cluster of competing social and governmental expectations and exigencies surrounding that right, or because of a blurriness as to what that right might encompass, or because of a lack of mechanisms to actually enforce it – then the argument here is that the right might as well not exist at all.

However, even though there may be no immediate enforceability of the right to privacy within the UNCRC, or any of the rights outlined in that convention (except where they already exist within domestic law), the UNCRC serves an important function – although perhaps not strictly a legal one. That is, by clearly setting out such rights, enforceable or otherwise, documents such as the UNCRC help to articulate two very important issues: first, they speak to the conceptualisation of the 'child' and the boundaries that constitute childhood. Second, they provide a vocabulary for concerns when different social, economic and governmental imperatives put pressure upon those boundaries. Arguably, lack of remedies aside, the UNCRC sets out an important symbolic benchmark for framing the debates around childhood; it puts children's privacy squarely on the table, and forces other imperatives, rationalities and mandates to factor it into their calculations. In this way, the UNCRC has rightly been described as an 'aspirational document'. While this may sound like a positive step, Rayner (2003, p. 28) also argues that this must be understood within the context of:

> children's continued powerlessness, low status, unjust treatment, abandonment, neglect and maltreatment, after a quarter century of reform. The UN *Convention on the Rights of the Child* may be an aspirational document, but it is also a benchmark of the value we really place on children in public life: not very high, and not very dear.

References

Bessant, J. & Watts, R. (2008) Children and the Law: an historical overview, in G. Monahan & L. Young (Eds) *Children and the Law in Australia.* Chatswood, NSW: LesisNexis Butterworths.

Borkowski, A. (1994) *Textbook on Roman Law.* London: Blackstone Press.

Burke, J. (1978) *Connections.* New York: Simon & Schuster.

Commonwealth Government of Australia (1988) Privacy Act.

Donzelot, J. (1979) *The Policing of Families.* New York: Pantheon Books.

Dresbeck, L. (1971) *The Chimney and Social Change in Medieval England.* New York: Elmira College.

Farson, R. (1974) *Birthrights.* New York: Collier Macmillan.

Fernando, M. (2013) Express Recognition of the UN Convention on the Rights of the Child in the Family Law Act: what impact for children's participation? *UNSW Law Journal,* 36(1), 88-106.

Foucault, M. (1997) *Discipline and Punish: the birth of the prison.* London: Penguin.

Foucault, M. (2001) Governmentality, in G. Burchell, C. Gordon & P. Miller (Eds) *The Foucault Effect: studies in governmentality.* London: Harvester Wheatsheaf.

Government of Victoria, Australia (1864) Neglected and Criminal Children's Act 1864 (Vic).

Hacking, I. (1982) Bio-power and the Avalanche of Printed Numbers, *Humanities and Society,* 5, 279-295.

Holt, J. (1975) *Escape from Childhood.* Harmondsworth: Penguin.

Jarzombek, M. (2010) Corridor Spaces, *Critical Inquiry,* 36, 728-770. http://dx.doi.org/10.1086/655210

Lansdown, G. (1994) Children's Rights, in B. Mayall (Ed.) *Children's Childhoods: observed and experienced.* London: Falmer Press.

Lansdown, G. (2005) *The Evolving Capacities of the Child.* Florence: UNICEF Innocenti Research Centre.

League of Nations (1924) Geneva Convention.

Locke, J. (1689) *Second Treatise of Civil Government.* London: Awnsham Churchill.

Marwick, A., Margia-Diaz, D. & Palfrey, J. (2010) *Youth, Privacy and Reputation:* literature review. Harvard University Public Law Working Papers, No. 10-29.

Mitchell, M. (2014) Children's Week 2014: discussion on the UNCRC 25 years on and the right to be heard, *Introduction to Children Week,* Monday 20 October. Canberra, Australia.

Paton, G. (2014) Classrooms Put Under Permanent Surveillance by CCTV, *Daily Telegraph,* 20 April.

Postman, N. (1994) *The Disappearance of Childhood*, 2nd edn. London: W.H. Allen.

Rayner, M. (2003) Why Children Need to Know Their Rights, *Newcastle Law Review*, 5(2), 23-35.

Rengel, A. (2013) *Privacy in the 21st Century*. Boston, MA: Leiden.

Rose, N. (1990) *Governing the Soul: the shaping of the private self*. London: Routledge.

Rose, N. & Miller, P. (1992) Political Power Beyond the State: problematics of government, *British Journal of Sociology*, 43(2), 173-205. http://dx.doi.org/10.2307/591464

Schapiro, T. (2003) Childhood and Personhood, *Arizona Law Review*, 45, 575-594.

Schoeman, F. (1980) Rights of Families: rights of parent, and the moral basis of the family, *Ethics*, 91, 6-19. http://dx.doi.org/10.1086/292199

Shmueli, B. & Blecher-Prigat, A. (2011) Privacy for Children, *Columbia Human Rights Law Review*, 42(3), 759-795.

Solove, D. (2008) *Understanding Privacy*. Cambridge, MA: Harvard University Press.

Spacks, P. (2003) *Privacy: concealing the eighteenth-century self*. Chicago: University of Chicago Press. http://dx.doi.org/10.7208/chicago/9780226768618.001.0001

Stockman, J. (2013) Big Data's Deal: the power pattern in collective human behaviour, *Boston Globe*, 18 June.

Tait, G. (2000) From the Panopticon to the Playground, in B. Burnett, D. Meadmore & G. Tait (Eds) *New Questions for Contemporary Teachers*. Frenches Forest, NSW: Pearson.

Tait, G. (2001) 'No Touch' Policies and the Management of Risk, in A. Jones (Ed.) *Touchy Subject: teachers touching children*. Dunedin: Otago Press.

Tannsjo, T. (2002) *Understanding Ethics: an introduction to moral theory*. Edinburgh: Edinburgh University Press.

Thomas, N. (2011) *Children's Rights: policy into practice*. Centre for Children and Young People: Background Briefing Series, No. 4. Lismore, NSW: Southern Cross University.

Tobin, J. (2008) The Development of Children's Rights, in G. Monahan & L. Young (Eds) *Children and the Law in Australia*. Chatswood, NSW: LesisNexis Butterworths.

United Kingdom Government (1998) Human Rights Act.

United Nations (1948) Universal Declaration on Human Rights.

United Nations (1959) Declaration on the Rights of the Child.

United Nations (1989) Convention on the Rights of the Child.

Warren, D. & Brandeis, L. (1890) The Right to Privacy, *Harvard Law Review*, 4, 193. http://dx.doi.org/10.2307/1321160

Wickham, G. (1993) Citizenship, Governance and the Consumption of Sport. Paper presented at the Australian Sociological Association Conference at Macquarie University, December, Sydney.

Wittgenstein, L. (1952) *Philosophical Investigations*, ed. G. Anscombe and R. Rhees. Oxford: Blackwell.

CHAPTER 7

The Future of Children's Rights, Educational Research and the UNCRC in a Digital World: possibilities and prospects

JENNA GILLETT-SWAN & VICKI COPPOCK

SUMMARY This chapter provides a critical discussion of how the UNCRC can shape methodological practices in educational research and how existing practices may be influenced with the ready access to, and development of, digital technologies. Key issues surrounding how the UNCRC is and should be informing educational research practices are discussed and contextualised within ethical and methodological positionings. In utilising a children's rights frame, this chapter further explores the opportunities and tensions that the UNCRC creates for educational researchers. While the availability of technology may increase the potential for actualising participatory methods that are more responsive to the methods that children seek to engage with in their free time, it also presents a number of challenges from an ethical and methodological standpoint. Technology changes the way in which individuals and communities interact with one another and the outside world. Both children's and adults' everyday lifeworlds are filled with a balance between the 'real' world and the cyber world and as the line between these two worlds is increasingly blurred, new opportunities for researchers seeking to understand children's lifeworlds in different contexts may be presented.

The ways in which children's rights are considered, conceptualised and enacted have changed significantly during the past 25 years, due in no small part to the influence and impact of the United Nations Convention on the Rights of the Child (United Nations, 1989) (hereafter CRC). Even so, as evidenced and explored throughout the preceding chapters, debate continues about how and the extent to which the children's rights agenda is embraced within education, as researchers, teachers and other educational professionals grapple with the work of translating the CRC into their daily practices. The landscape of children's rights is ever-changing, and with the increased incorporation and widespread use of technology, it presents a range of opportunities and challenges for educational researchers now and into the future. Therefore, in this concluding chapter we discuss some of the emerging issues and debates surrounding children's rights, educational research, and the CRC in the modern digital world.

Within educational contexts there is a dearth of academic research on children, young people and digital media conducted from a children's human rights–informed perspective (Moyle & Owen, 2009; Brown, 2012; Moyle et al, 2012). Rather, the emerging literature in this area is mainly located in the cultural, media studies and ICT fields (see Livingstone et al, 2011; boyd, 2014). Our aim here is to begin to redress this absence. In distinguishing between protection, provision and participation rights as they relate to educational research and digital media, we contextualise our discussion within the mandates of the CRC, highlighting opportunities, tensions and emerging issues in a field that is complicated, under-researched and highly topical (Livingstone & O'Neill, 2014). In this sense, the intention is to map current concerns and also lay the groundwork for future exploration and development of the field of digital media and children's rights and the CRC in educational contexts.

The Digital Child: contexts, scope and significance

The exponential growth and significance of digital technologies since the turn of the twenty-first century, particularly the rapid expansion and development of social media platforms, is staggering. For example, according to statistics provided by Digital Insights (2014), Facebook has 1.28 billion monthly active users, YouTube 1 billion, Google+ 540 million, Twitter 255 million and Instagram 200 million – 23% of teens citing the latter as their favourite social network. In a survey of over 25,000 children and young people aged between 9 and 16 across 25 European countries, Livingstone et al (2011) found that children of this age are highly engaged with social media. Of the 9- to 12-year-olds in the study, 38% maintained a social networking profile, along with 77% of the 13- to 16-year-olds. Facebook was used by one third of 9-16-year-old Internet users, with 1 in 5 children aged between 9 and 12 having a Facebook profile, even 4 in 10 children in some countries. This is despite popular social networking platforms such as Facebook having minimum age membership requirements of 13 years old. A more recent study in the United States determined that more than 70% of teenagers used Facebook, with over 90% accessing online content on a daily basis

(Lenhart & Pew Research Center, 2015). Evidently social media and the Internet are popular with today's young people.

According to Livingstone and Bober (2004, p. 9):

> In strikingly few years, children have rapidly gained access to the internet at both school and home, strongly supported by Government policy and industry initiatives. Indeed, young people's lives are increasingly mediated by information and communication technologies – at home, at schools and in the community.

Interestingly, however, the boundaries between and across these different contexts may be blurred, indicating that children's digital media use may not be as easily differentiable within their lifeworld. As Brown (2012) reports, 'students did not see clear boundaries between the use of digital technologies in and outside of school. For them, these domains [a]re inexorably linked' (p. 125).

Researchers in the cultural, media studies and ICT fields have offered valuable insights into the 'ways that social and cultural shifts created by digital technologies have transformed our relationships to (and definitions of) place, culture, politics and infrastructure' (Varnelis, 2008, para 1). Drawing on her extensive ethnographic research into the social lives of networked teens in the United States, boyd (2014) observes how social media plays a crucial role in the lives of networked children and young people and has become an important public space where they can gather and socialise with peers in an informal way. Their engagement with digital technologies increasingly mediates their lives, experiences and opportunities. She describes how children and young people's desire for connection and autonomy is now being expressed in 'networked publics', which she explains is 'simultaneously (1) the space constructed though networked technologies and (2) the imagined community that emerges as a result of the intersection of people, technology and practice' (boyd, 2014, p. 8).

The theorisation developed by boyd, and others in this field, resonates with themes and issues of concern for research on children's rights in education. Three themes in particular can be highlighted – identity, peer sociality, and power relations. Children's identities are both reflected and formed through networked spaces. As Fraser (1992) describes, 'publics ... are arenas for the formation and enactment of social identities' (p. 68) where children and young people are increasingly choosing these platforms to display how they want to be represented publicly. This representation may be one version of 'self' as portrayed by the online persona which may not be representative of an individual's 'real' self. Peer sociality in publics 'emerge[s] when audiences come together around shared understandings of the world' (Livingstone, 2005, p. 9), where individuals co-construct meaning and identity based on their interactions and exhibition of how they want to be perceived in their social worlds. As with the power-relations hierarchy embedded within 'real-life' childhood, these power relations also occur in the online digital space and can serve to either empower or further marginalise those who may be already marginalised in the non-digital world. As Warner describes, 'counter-publics enable marginalised individuals to create powerful communities in resistance to hegemonic publics' (cited in boyd, 2014, p. 222) which can empower individuals in different contexts. This in turn can make the 'powerless' in one context more powerful in another, therefore providing multiple representations of the self that play out differently in alternate (and multiple) realities – online and offline.

Networked publics appeal to children and young people because, as boyd (2014) describes, they 'want to be part of the broader world by connecting with others and having freedom of mobility' (p. 10) and they want to do so *on their own terms*, which is something that is more easily enabled by digital technologies. When it comes to children's civic participation, boyd (2014) describes adult apprehension of digital technology and its capacity for enabling children's citizenship and the development of autonomy, which can be confronting or intimidating for some. Clearly this is a rich terrain for those of us seeking to interrogate and understand the scope, significance and limitations of children's rights theory, policy and practice in educational contexts.

Digital Media, Children's Rights and the CRC

The role and importance of the mass media in promoting human rights was first established in 1978 with the UNESCO Declaration. Article IV of the Declaration relates to children and young people. The importance of media engagement in promoting children's human rights was further established in Article 17 of the CRC, which mandates for a child's 'access to information and material from a diverse range of national and international sources, especially those aimed at the promotion of his or her social, spiritual and moral well-being and physical and mental health' (United Nations, 1989). More recently, considerations around children's rights and digital media have become a prominent area of focus for the United Nations Committee on the Rights of the Child, which devoted a Day of General Discussion exclusively to this topic on 12 September 2014. This discussion sought to 'analyse the effects of children's engagement with social media and information and communications technologies (ICTs), in order to better understand the impact on and role of children's rights in this area, and develop rights-based strategies to maximize the online opportunities for children while protecting them from risks and possible harm without restricting any benefits' (United Nations, 2014, p. 2).

Fayoyin (2011) outlines three broad assertions when considering the relationship between the CRC, children's rights and digital media which map directly onto the extensively used conceptual framework of the CRC's '3 Ps'. First, digital media promotes access to, and utilisation of, key education, health and social services (Provision). Second, digital media holds considerable prospects for empowering children and young people to become informed and active advocates of their rights (Participation). Finally, digital media also comes with considerable challenges that have a bearing on the potential for violation of children's rights (Protection). Livingstone (cited in United Nations, 2014, p. 4) argues that, when it comes to the CRC and digital media,

> [e]mphasis should be on the right to protection from harm, the right to provision to meet needs and the right to participation as an agent, or citizen. The task at hand [is] therefore to identify where, when and how the Internet reconfigured the conditions of harm, need and agency.

However, there is an obvious tension between using digital media for the advancement of children's rights through increased, less-mediated participation opportunities, and seeking to protect the child from the short-, medium-, and long-term realities (and permanence) of the online, digital space. Thus, as Livingstone and O'Neill (2014, p. 23) observe:

> Two broad strategies have emerged – a regulatory approach that transposes individual rights and preventative measures into appropriate legal or other (self- or co-) regulatory instruments, and a broader policy approach that focuses on child wellbeing, emphasising appropriate provision for children and support for their participation.

These approaches also transcend into the domain of educational research, where different approaches to understanding the complexities of children's lifeworld in different contexts are presented.

Digital Media and Children's Rights in Education

Provision Rights

Discussions around children's rights, research and digital media are becoming increasingly relevant in educational contexts as digital technology has become an important part of children's daily lives, both at home and at school (Livingstone & Bober, 2004; Brown, 2012; Kolikant, 2012; Swist et al, 2015). There has been an exponential increase in the use of digital media in educational practices, among which social media and networking sites often feature (Livingstone & Bober, 2004; Brown, 2012; Kolikant, 2012; Digital Education Advisory Group, 2013; OECD 2015; Swist et al, 2015). Examples such as virtual study groups and communities of practice to enhance student learning through software such as Edmodo, Saywire, Edublogs, Skype, Google+ and other creative commons applications enable children and young people to be more connected to each other as well as to the world around them (Varlas, 2011). Children and young people are using technology to take responsibility for their own learning through being able to personalise their learning experiences according to their learning styles and interests (Brown, 2012; Kolikant, 2012; Digital Education Advisory Group, 2013; Carrington, 2015; OECD 2015). As Livingstone and O'Neill (2014, p. 26) maintain:

> Increasingly, educators argue that digital competence as an essential skill for life-long learning represents a vital contemporary extension of the right to education, requiring governments and other agencies to make appropriate provision for the development of children's full potential in the digital age.

In this sense, it is argued that digital and social media are contributing to a shift in educational practice from a transmissional or transactional learning paradigm to a transformative learning paradigm. The significance of this is illustrated by Kalantzis and Cope (2010, p. 203):

> A previous generation became literate by reading in their spare time. Generation P [participatory] becomes literate by writing in their spare time – on Facebook, Twitter, blogs and even text messaging. A previous generation passively watched television programming that others considered good for them on a handful of available channels. Generation P 'channel surfs' hundreds of channels, or the millions of videos on YouTube, or makes their own videos – on the phones even – and uploads them to YouTube. This generation will be frustrated by a curriculum which expects them to be passive recipients of formal, generic textbook content.

It is also argued that children's engagement with social media and other technologies offers opportunities and contexts within which their psychosocial development is supported (Mallan et al, 2010; Third et al, 2014; Swist et al, 2015).

Participation Rights

In considering the scope for social media to enhance children's rights, it is suggested that they may empower children through providing tools and awareness of digital literacy, citizenship, freedom of expression, right to privacy and respecting the rights of others (Council of Europe, 2014). Social media can also promote children's rights education through the right to information (Articles 13 and 17), as well as by making the CRC known (Article 42). Examples include the Google + Hangout hosted by the UN Committee on the Rights of the Child on the 25th anniversary of the CRC [1] and the use of Pinterest by students at the Ajman Academy in the United Arab Emirates to illustrate 'The Face of Advocacy Through the Eyes of Children in Dubai'.[2]

Social media can enable freedom of expression (Articles 12 and 13) and have 'considerable prospects for empowering young people to becoming informed and active advocates of their rights while reducing the tokenism that has characterised their engagement in child rights advocacy programming' (Fayoyin, 2011, p. 57). As Richardson (2011) suggests, 'Social media afford the opportunity for all children with online access to contribute to the world in meaningful ways' (p.26), which aids in enabling their citizenship and their ability to enact social change (Fayoyin, 2011). There are numerous examples of pupils as both 'passionate participants' and 'change agents' (Richardson, 2011). Perhaps the most notable of these in recent times is education campaigner and 2014 Nobel Peace Prize winner Malala Yousafzai, who has used digital and social media extensively in her efforts to raise awareness of and promote children's rights globally (see, for example, *We Are Silent*.[3] Similarly, UNICEF's *Voices of Youth* offers children and young people globally a digital space and online community within which they can share their views on issues of concern to them (see, for example, *Tweet Up Your Mind!*[4]

Protection Rights

Despite these positive aspects, some governments are now seeking to restrict children's access to social media, as witnessed in proposed changes to European data legislation (European Commission, 2012, 2015). The proposed changes take a firm stance on the protection of young people from social media through disallowing children and young people under the age of 16 to use these and similar Internet sites (European Commission, 2012, 2015; Titcomb, 2015). The protection of children when they are provided with ready access to information is an important consideration but, as is frequently the case in the field of children's rights, there is an obvious tension between healthy protectionism and unhealthy paternalism that risks undermining the scope for enhancing children's status as autonomous 'beings'.

Unsurprisingly, issues around children's protection rights tend to dominate popular, political and academic discourse, providing direct connections to Articles 17e, 19, 34, and 36 of the CRC. The dominant focus of these discussions is on 'risk' and 'danger' online through, for example, sexual exploitation, cyber bullying and addiction (Longe & Longe, 2009; Fayoyin, 2011; Council of Europe, 2014; Third et al, 2014).

Byron argues that children 'are more vulnerable there [online] than if they were hanging out on the street' (cited in Woods, 2013, para 22). This discourse has generated new legal and policy responses through child protection structures and, in Europe, the Safer Internet Programme. Fayoyin (2011) comments that 'while the new media affords the opportunity for the promotion of participation and protection rights' (p. 62), it also presents challenges around the manifestation of 'some dysfunctional effects in terms of exposing children and young people to information that may be potentially harmful to their holistic development ... [and around] the cognitive, physical and social development of the children' (p. 62). Byron (2008, p. 3) also expresses concerns around the impact of technologies on children's development, such as through bullying and 'excessive use ... at the expense of other activities and family interaction ... [and] taking risks in the digital world'.

The potential risk for the private lives of children is also highlighted where information they have disclosed through their engagement with technology as a means of socialisation can be used years later by educational institutions or potential future employers. Children have access to and are producers of large-scale uncensored information that is easily and widely accessible and distributable, which may have significant ramifications in children's futures. Even now, teachers are being reprimanded for their online presence during the years of their youth when technology was significantly less developed than it is in its current form. The effects on children's futures of revealing children's private lives was identified by the Council of Europe's Commissioner for Human Rights' comment (Council of Europe, 2014), 'Protecting Children's Rights in the Digital World: an ever-growing challenge', in that:

> Teenagers spend a substantial share of their time on Internet,
> often using social media, which have become a major means of
> socialising. Growing access to the Internet has brought about
> almost unlimited possibilities for children to access content
> and exercise their rights, including the right to receive and
> impart information. However these benefits go hand in hand
> with growing risks for children of violations of their rights.

The profiling of information and retention of data regarding children's activities on the Internet for commercial purposes also raises privacy concerns to which children are mostly not sensitised, such as, for example, the controversial 'Facebook experiment' (Kramer et al, 2014) where the Facebook news feeds of 689,003 Facebook users were manipulated without user consent. The users' subsequent posts and reactions were then examined to determine whether the type of news presented through a social network (positive or negative) influenced an individual's emotional responses. No demographic details of participants were reported (for example, age, gender or nationality), and only those 'who viewed Facebook in English were qualified for selection into the experiment' (Kramer et al, 2014, p. 8788). From a children's rights standpoint, this study may have included (and likely did include) children under the age of 18 who may require additional protections associated with their age and relative vulnerability. As the experiment did not follow standard university ethical consent procedures (it was given an ethical exemption due to the Facebook terms of use agreement), it is questionable as to whether any participants whose Facebook feeds were manipulated were provided with any follow-up care or access to support services. Facebook requires its members to be aged 13 or older; however, as described earlier, many studies have found children younger than this holding accounts, with suggestions that over 7.5 million children under the age of 13 are also Facebook members (Varlas, 2011).

New Technologies, Same Old Issues and Tensions?

While the digital technologies and platforms are 'new', the tensions and contradictions surrounding children's rights to provision, protection and participation to which they relate are not. For example, when considering the role of social media as enhancers of children's participation rights, we need to question the extent to which they really can, and do, 'empower' children, as is often claimed. Initial complications emerge around considerations of the potential 'empowerment' of children through digital technologies and social media when we ask the question, 'Which children?' While the 'digital revolution' has oft been hailed as a force for global democratisation, issues concerning access and equity remain. Discussions about the opportunities and challenges presented through children's increased access to technology and information tend to be dominated by a focus on the global North. This imposes certain cultural and value-laden assumptions that are not necessarily applicable or relevant to children in other contexts (Livingstone, cited in United Nations, 2014). Arguably, the focus for children in less developed countries may be more attuned to achieving their basic fundamental needs and survival, than, for example, being concerned with age restrictions on various social media platforms. Even in developed countries, the extent of personal empowerment fulfilled through technology and technological access is unable to be generalised for all western childhoods. This brings into question the circumstances around children's participation and 'empowerment' through technology, as well as how and why this occurs.

Further issues arise when we ask, 'Participation for what?' Children's online participation may serve many purposes, including enabling greater citizenship, demonstrating responsibility, and political engagement. It may, however, purely represent a tokenism for presenting positive societal perceptions, such as is demonstrated through UNICEF's 2013 'Likes Don't Save Lives' campaign. This campaign satirises individual diffusion of responsibility and action through social media and uses examples of 'likes' on social media taking the place of personal action and commitment, but amounting to little other than in-principle support. Technology breeding complacency and tokenism may therefore transcend to children's domains where generations of 'likers' rather than 'doers' are formed, developing a society of passive recipients rather than facilitators of action, empowerment and social change.

As in most other areas of social life, adults routinely mediate children's online 'voices' and, therefore, limit their autonomy and 'freedom' to participate. While seeking to enable the protection of children online, these protections also perpetuate restrictive management practices where adults block and filter content that could then be argued to deny children the right to access information as provided through Articles 13 and 17. As Fayoyin (2011) explains, 'underlying the principle of protection is the notion of the evolving capacity of children' [Article 5] (p. 60), which Lansdown (2005) argues is typically correlated with the age and maturity of the child, with 'the assumption that competence correlates with age [which] is widely used to justify restrictions on children' (p. 28).

What then are the limits to children's agency online, and where do 'we', as adults, researchers, teachers, support staff, parents and others involved in children's lives, draw the line to this agency? The lines become blurred as to whose role and responsibility it is to mediate and control this space, and at what point this 'protection' becomes censorship. We refer, for example, to digitally aided education and considerations around the extent to which teachers, researchers and those involved with children and childhood can monitor, protect and censor (when necessary) what children do when using their own devices in educational contexts and for educational tasks. On the one hand, there is a push in education for acknowledgement and incorporation of the tools and resources that children seek to engage with in their own time as a way to increase engagement and motivation. On the other hand, however, as Tait and Tambyah (this volume) point out, parameters around children's right to privacy could be questioned, which may then lead to the boundaries between a teacher's duty-of-care requirements and children's right to expression, information and participation being blurred. This is exemplified in recent controversial reforms in schools in England requiring teachers to monitor pupils' Internet use in order to prevent radicalisation (*BBC News*, 2015).

Issues around children's right to privacy (Articles 8 and 16) also come to the fore when considering parents who post videos and pictures of their children online. Parents are usually those held responsible for ensuring the protection of their child/children in the wider online space.

(This is particularly true with the implementation of the new European data legislation, as discussed earlier [European Commission, 2012, 2015]). Yet, many are freely sharing images of their own and friends' children through their own (social) networks. In many instances, the short- and long-term ramifications of 'sharing' online are not considered, including the permanence of the online space and possible future consequences for the child (Lombardi, 2013). The future consequences of material posted online are hotly debated, with discussions around the inclusion of a 'right to be forgotten' occurring at high levels of government in the European Union and the United Kingdom (European Commission, 2015). There remains a tension once more as to where the line is drawn between an individual's right to privacy and the right of the public/community to information, which can then be used for public good, and the public interest, including 'remind[ing] all stakeholders that what happens offline today, will also be manifest online and what happens online has consequences offline' (Livingstone, cited in United Nations, 2014, p. 4). Other issues, such as managing boundaries between staff and students, including to the extent that students, staff and schools should utilise social media to be 'friends', present another layer of complexity to an already complex issue where the boundaries between privacy, transparency and communicating in ways of an individual's choosing are blurred.

Further implications of online sharing of information and images for teachers, children and young people involve possible legal action. 'The Tweet that Cost $105,000' (*Sydney Morning Herald*, 2015 [see Whitbourn, 2014]); police involvement ('Girl, 13, Reported to Police by Her School For Taking a Snapchat Picture of Her Teacher During a Lesson' [*Daily Mail*, 2015]); and dismissal/expulsion ('Teacher Sacked for Posting Picture of Herself Holding Glass of Wine and Mug of Beer on Facebook' [*Daily Mail*, 2011]): these are all examples of situations that are becoming increasingly common. But situations such as schools banning parents taking photos of their children at school events, children being reported to police for taking photos in class, and the extent of parents' access to children's emails and texts all represent opportunities for conversations with different stakeholders around contemporary issues in this space of children's rights, digital media, and protection of children. Careful consideration of the balance between participation and protection in these situations provides fruitful opportunities for future educational research that seeks to investigate children's rights issues in practice in educational settings.

All of these issues warrant careful investigation and consideration. Yet the tendency has veered towards moral panic around the perils of digital media and the demonisation and pathologising of its effects. Sensationalised and highly emotive media coverage such as, on the *BBC News*, 'Do We Need to Rescue Our Kids from the Digital World?'

(Wakefield, 2014); in the *Telegraph*, 'Toddlers Becoming So Addicted to iPads They Require Therapy' (Ward, 2013); and in *The Times*, 'Don't Panic ... Empower Your Child Online' (Gibbons, 2014), present a harmful and scaremongering view of technology and its effects.

boyd (2014) observes a tendency towards 'technological determinism' (p. 15) – that is, an 'assumption that technologies possess intrinsic powers that affect all people in all situations the same way' (p. 15). She suggests that exaggerated fears around digital technologies are reminiscent of societal reactions to technological innovations in earlier historical periods, such as the development of the printing press. It seems that when children are involved, protectionism becomes the default position and trumps the right to participation and autonomy. Thus, boyd argues, it is easier to focus on the technology than on the broader systemic issues at play in children's lives, such as the negative impacts of gendered, racial and socio-economic inequalities. Her research reveals that many of the much-hyped concerns around children's engagement with digital and social media may be misleading and counterproductive, serving as distractions from 'real' risks to children. Indeed, she warns, 'we spend so much time worrying about children and young people that we fail to account for how our paternalism and protectionism hinders their ability to become informed, thoughtful and engaged adults' (boyd, 2014, p. 28).

Using Digital and Social Media to Promote Children's Rights–informed Research Practices

Given the scope and complexity of the issues surrounding children's rights and digital/social media discussed above, it seems obvious that educational researchers might be put off from engaging with these technologies in their research. When exercising methodological choices, consideration of the use of digital technologies and social media platforms may seem daunting, posing an additional hurdle for those seeking to understand the changing face of educational research from a rights-based perspective. Nevertheless, there are opportunities for utilising digital technologies in engaging with children and young people in ways that respect their privacy, provide protection and enable their participation, as, for example, in projects such as *Young Digital*.[5] This is a useful resource for anyone interested in using digital media for research, consultation or participation activities with children and young people. Advice and information is available on technical aspects of using digital media in research with children; choosing methods; ethical issues and how to deal with them; analysis and dissemination with digital media; and involving children and young people as co-producers of knowledge. Other examples of inter-disciplinary projects seeking to develop the research base around children's rights and digital technologies in rights-friendly and rights-inclusive ways include *Global Kids Online*, *EU Kids Online*, *iRights* and the *Young and Well Cooperative Research Centre*.

The use of digital and social media in research may pose specific ethical challenges for educational researchers. For example, the ability to access children's 'private' thoughts and reflections when they publicly share on social media can be a slippery slope. The permanence of the digital form offers additional complexities to an increasingly complex balance between privacy, protection, vulnerability and expression. When the Convention on the Rights of the Child was created, the Internet was still in its early stages. With the exponential growth and expansion of technology and its capabilities, those involved in developing the Convention would have had little insight as to what the provisions for children's 'access to information' and 'freedom of expression' may mean in a technologically advanced society. Parsons and Abbott (2013) highlight some of the ways in which digital media can be used to enhance a rights-inclusive approach to research with children, arguing that it 'offers the potential to support the presentation of information about research topics and methodologies, and children's decision-making about their own participation, more effectively than by traditional, often paper-based, methods' (p. 1). In considering the affordances of digital technologies in supporting informed consent with children, they outline three dimensions of participation in which digital technologies could play an important role: '(i) *accessibility* of information presented for improved comprehension; (ii) *motivation* to take part in the research and (iii) *competence and autonomy* to make and express an informed decision' (p. 2). Nevertheless, while the digital world may represent a different research milieu, it could be questioned whether the ethical challenges presented are substantively different from non-technological research approaches. It is important to remember that the principles of good ethical conduct in research with children and young people transcend the research context (Sargeant & Harcourt, 2012).

Digital media are certainly transforming academia where 'traditional' approaches to academic research, publication and dissemination, each with their own associated power elites and structures, are increasingly being challenged in the digital age. This provides immense scope for the educational researcher in terms of global networking and collaboration through communities of researchers, discovering new interdisciplinary connections, enabling much wider dissemination of research, providing continual and faster peer review, and facilitating different forms of research output. There is both a need and an opportunity to move research on children's rights in education forward in the digital age – to explore possibilities in relation to 'new' research questions, research practices, research communities and research dissemination.

Conclusion

This edited collection has drawn together contributions from around the world to represent the global context, relevance and implications of children's rights, educational research and the CRC from multiple perspectives. Examples from Australia, Sweden, Finland, the United Kingdom and Portugal have provided diverse and wide-ranging contexts within which different aspects of children's rights are problematised and interesting implications and considerations for educational and research practice explored. Many of the issues discussed become increasingly complex when adding the expansion of digital technology and access to media into the equation. Educational practice has seen substantial growth in the integration and inclusion of digital technologies, such as social media, in response to meeting the needs of a twenty-first-century learner or 'digital native' (Prensky, 2001). The potential of such technologies is cautiously approached and may be underdeveloped when considering the future of children's rights in education and how the CRC may be acted upon. For example, Phillips' (this volume) discussion of the limited impact of national and international children's rights education programmes highlights the potential for the use of digital media in publicly promoting the CRC in order that children might know and claim their rights in accordance with Article 42. To this end, media and technological access is viewed as an enabler and an opportunity for children's participatory, expressive and citizenship rights to be enacted. However, as Tait and Tambyah (this volume) caution, children's right to privacy (Article 16) can become increasingly problematic in contexts where children's increased access to information and exposure to wider audiences without censorship may create additional legal, moral and ethical dilemmas for those seeking to both understand and protect children. Such conflicts and tensions are of growing significance for both educators and educational researchers and cannot be ignored.

There are many examples where technology is being used successfully to engage with children, families and the community in sharing, such as children in kindergarten using social networking to share their classroom activities with the school, community and general public. Technology use and incorporation assists in developing children's communities focused around their interests (Steward et al, 2011), and both enables communication between different people which would not be possible without technology (Bonetti et al, 2010) as well as providing the ability to learn about a range of people (Bonetti et al, 2010). Technology may also enable the development of closer relationships with friends and family (Valkenburg & Peter, 2007; Lee, 2009) and social skill development and support (Bryant et al, 2006; Leung, 2007; Valkenburg & Peter, 2007), as well as providing positive effects to mental health (Valkenburg et al, 2006; Valkenburg & Peter, 2007). Each of these are arguably positive effects that can be better enabled and facilitated with the incorporation of technology in educational practice and the acknowledgement of its beneficial potential in research. However, a consideration of some of the cons, such as cyber-bullying (Juvonen & Gross, 2008), unfavourable social comparison (Qui et al, 2012), less 'human' contact and face-to-face communication (Lee, 2009; Bonetti et al, 2010), encouraging and normalising risky behaviours (Moreno et al, 2009; Huang et al, 2012), brings into question what this accessibility may mean for the future of children's rights and the future of educational research, and, indeed, for the relevance of the Convention on the Rights of the Child in today's society.

As boyd's (2014) publication so aptly describes, *'It's Complicated'*, and complicated is certainly where the issues remain. Even so, current knowledge and understanding of social media in the lives of children and young people is comparatively limited and partial, which can (and does) lead to many misassumptions. The nuanced realities of children and young people's interactions with social media are full of both pros and cons, adding increased complexity to the role of educational researchers in seeking to enable children's rights, understand children's lifeworlds and progress in a rapidly developing technological society. Nonetheless, educational researchers in the twenty-first century increasingly need to be skilled in the use of digital media and aware of the ethical issues and challenges involved in order to maintain children's rights–informed research practice into the future.

Finally, we are reminded that 'children around the world increasingly think of access to digital media as a fundamental right' (Third et al, 2014, p. 8), which demonstrates that digital media are important to them and, *from their perspectives*, an important aid to enacting their rights. If, as educational researchers, we are committed to taking children's rights seriously, it is vital that we, as powerful adults, facilitate continuous, open dialogue with children about their use of digital media and seek *their views* on how it can best be harnessed to serve their rights, now and into the future.

Notes

[1] https://plus.google.com/events/c6gkj3n3gf7nk07eveljd6av6qo

[2] https://uk.pinterest.com/MOMentumNation/the-face-of-advocacy-through-the-eyes-of-children-/

[3] http://www.weday.com/we-schools/campaigns/we-are-silent/

[4] http://www.voicesofyouth.org/en/posts/tweet-up-your-mind-

[5] http://www.youngdigital.net

References

BBC News (2015) Schools Told to Monitor Pupils' Web Use to Prevent Radicalisation. 22 December. http://www.bbc.co.uk/news/uk-35157910 (accessed 22 January 2016).

Bonetti, L., Campbell, M.A. & Gilmore, L. (2010) The Relationship of Oneliness and Social Anxiety with Children's and Adolescents' Online Communication, *CyberPsychology, Behavior, and Social Networking*, 13, 279-285. http://dx.doi.org/10.1089/cyber.2009.0215

boyd, d. (2014) *It's Complicated: the social lives of networked teens.* Newhaven, CT: Yale University Press.

Brown, B. (2012) Student Voices and Digital Technologies in Australian School Education, in K. Moyle & G. Wijngaards (Eds) *Student Reactions to Learning with Technologies: perceptions and outcomes*, pp. 117-141. Hershey, PA: IGI Global Publications.

Bryant, J.A., Sanders-Jackson, A. & Smallwood, A.M.K. (2006) IMing, text messaging, and adolescent social networks, *Journal of Computer-mediated Communication*, 11(2), 577-592. http://dx.doi.org/10.1111/j.1083-6101.2006.00028.x

Byron, T. (2008) Safer Children in a Digital World: the report of the Byron Review. Children and New Technology. http://webarchive.nationalarchives.gov.uk/20100113232942/http://dcsf.gov.uk/byronreview/pdfs/Final%20Report%20Bookmarked.pdf

Carrington, A. (2015) The Pedagogy Wheel. http://www.unity.net.au/padwheel/padwheelposter.pdf (padagogy wheel) or http://www.unity.net.au/allansportfolio/wp/wp-content/uploads/2015/03/Wheel_only_V4_LowRez_650x650.jpg

Council of Europe (2014) Protecting Children's Rights in the Digital World: an ever-growing challenge. Commissioner for Human Rights' comment.

Daily Mail (2011) Teacher Sacked for Posting Picture of Herself Holding Glass of Wine and Mug of Beer on Facebook. http://www.dailymail.co.uk/news/article-1354515/Teacher-sacked-posting-picture-holding-glass-wine-mug-beer-Facebook.html (accessed 8 August 2014).

Daily Mail (2015) Girl, 13, Reported to Police by Her School For Taking a Snapchat Picture of Her Teacher During a Lesson, *Daily Mail Online*. http://www.dailymail.co.uk/news/article-3356377/Schoolgirl-13-reported-police-teachers-taking-Snapchat-picture-teacher-lesson-warned-face-criminal-charges.html (accessed 14 December 2015).

Digital Education Advisory Group (2013) Beyond the Classroom: a new digital education for young Australians in the 21st century.

Digital Insights (2014) http://blog.digitalinsights.in/social-media-users-2014-stats-numbers/05205287.html (accessed 16 July 2014).

European Commission (2012) Safeguarding Privacy in a Connected World: a European data protection framework for the 21st century. http://eur-lex.europa.eu/LexUriServ/LexUriServ. do?uri=COM:2012:0009:FIN:EN:PDF

European Commission (2015) Reform of EU Data Protection Rules. http://ec.europa.eu/justice/data-protection/reform/index_en.htm

Fayoyin, A. (2011) Promoting Children's Rights through the New Media: the Nigerian experience, *Journal of Communication*, 2(2), 57-65.

Fraser, N. (1992) Rethinking the Public Sphere: a contribution to the critique of actually existing democracy, in C. Calhoun (Ed.) *Habermas and the Public Sphere*. Cambridge, MA: MIT Press.

Gibbons, K. (2014) Don't Panic... Empower Your Child Online, *The Times*. http://www.thetimes.co.uk/tto/technology/internet/article4040179.ece

Huang, G.C., Okamoto, J., Valente, T.W., Sun, P., Wei, Y., Johnson, C.A. & Unger, J.B. (2012) Effects of Media and Social Standing on Smoking Behaviors among Adolescents in China, *Journal of Children and Media*, 6(1), 100-118. http://dx.doi.org/10.1080/17482798.2011.633411

Juvonen, J. & Gross, E.F. (2008). Extending the School Grounds? Bullying Experiences in Cyberspace, *Journal of School Health*, 78, 496-505. http://dx.doi.org/10.1111/j.1746-1561.2008.00335.x

Kalantzis, M. & Cope, B. (2010) The Teacher as Designer: pedagogy in the new media age, *e-Learning and Digital Media*, 7(3), 200-222.

Kolikant, B.D. (2012) Using ICT for School Purposes: is there a student-school disconnect?, *Computers and Education*, 59, 907-914. http://dx.doi.org/10.1016/j.compedu.2012.04.012

Kramer, A.D., Guillory, J.E. & Hancock, J.T. (2014) Experimental Evidence of Massive-scale Emotional Contagion through Social Networks, *Proceedings of the National Academy of Sciences*, 111(24), 8788-8790. http://dx.doi.org/10.1073/pnas.1320040111

Lansdown, G. (2005) *The Evolving Capacities of the Child*. Florence, Italy: UNICEF.

Lee, S.J. (2009) Online Communication and Adolescent Social Ties: who benefits more from internet use? *Journal of Computer-mediated Communication*, 14(3), 509-531. http://dx.doi.org/10.1111/j.1083-6101.2009.01451.x

Lenhart, A. & Pew Research Center (2015) *Teens, Social Media & Technology Overview 2015*. Washington, DC: Pew Research Center.

Leung, L. (2007) Stressful Life Events, Motives for Internet Use, and Social Support among Digital Kids, *Journal of CyberPsychology and Behavior*, 10(2), 204-214. http://dx.doi.org/10.1089/cpb.2006.9967

Livingstone, S. (2005) On the Relation between Audiences and Publics, in S. Livingstone (Ed.) *Audiences and Publics: when cultural engagement matters for the public sphere*. Bristol: Intellect Books.

Livingstone, S. & Bober, M. (2004) *UK Children Go Online: surveying the experiences of young people and their parents*. London: LSE Research Online. http://eprints.lse.ac.uk/395/1/UKCGOsurveyreport.pdf

Livingstone, S., Haddon, L., Görzig, A. & Ólafsson, K. (2011) *Risks and Safety on the Internet: the perspective of European children*. Full findings. London: LSE, EU Kids Online.

Livingstone, S. & O'Neill, B. (2014) Children's Rights Online: challenges, dilemmas and emerging directions, in S. van der Hof, B. van den Berg & B. Schermer (Eds) *Minding Minors Wandering the Web: Regulating Online Child Safety*, Information Technology and Law Series 24, 19-38. http://dx.doi.org/10.1007/978-94-6265-005-3_2

Lombardi, J. (2013) Going Viral: social media and your children's privacy, *You and Your Family, Development & Behavior*, Mom Stories, 6 November.

Longe, O.B. & Longe, F.A. (2009) The Nigerian Web Content: combating pornography using content filters, *Journal of Information Technology Impact*, 15(2), 59-64.

Mallan, K.M., Ashford, B. & Singh, P. (2010) Navigating iScapes: Australian youth constructing identities and social relations in a networked society, *Anthropology and Education Quarterly*, 41(3), 264-279. http://dx.doi.org/10.1111/j.1548-1492.2010.01087.x

Moreno, M.A., Vanderstoep, A., Parks, M.R., Zimmerman, F.J., Kurth, A. & Christakis, D.A. (2009) Reducing At-risk Adolescents' Display of Risk Behavior on a Social Networking Web Site: a randomized controlled pilot intervention trial, *Archives of Pediatrics and Adolescent Medicine*, 163, 35-41. http://dx.doi.org/10.1001/archpediatrics.2008.502

Moyle, K. & Owen, S. (2009) Listening to Students' and Educators' Voices: the views of students and early career educators about learning with technologies in Australian education and training. Research findings. Department of Education, Employment and Workplace Relations.

Moyle, K., Wijngaards, G. & Owen, S. (2012) Students' Views about Learning with Technologies: a literature review, in K. Moyle & G. Wijngaards (Eds) *Student Reactions to Learning with Technologies: perceptions and outcomes*. Hershey, PA: IGI Global Publications. http://dx.doi.org/10.4018/978-1-61350-177-1.ch001

Organisation for Economic Co-operation and Development (OECD) (2015) Teaching with Technology, *Teaching in Focus*, 12, 1-4.

Parsons, S. & Abbott, C. (2013) Digital Technologies for Supporting the Informed Consent of Children and Young People in Research: the potential for transforming current research ethics practice. Engineering and Physical Sciences Research Council (EPSRC) Observatory for Responsible Innovation in ICT. http://eprints.soton.ac.uk/356041/

Prensky, M. (2001) Digital Natives, Digital Immigrants. http://www.marcprensky.com/writing/Prensky%20-%20Digital%20Natives,%20Digital%20Immigrants%20-%20Part1.pdf

Qiu, L., Lin, H., Leung, A.K. & Tov, W. (2012) Putting Their Best Foot Forward: emotional disclosure on Facebook, *Journal of CyberPsychology, Behavior, and Social Networking*, 15(10), 569-572. http://dx.doi.org/10.1089/cyber.2012.0200

Richardson, W. (2011) Publishers, Participants All, *Educational Leadership*, 68(5), Teaching Screenagers, 22-26.

Sargeant, J. & Harcourt, D. (2012) *Doing Ethical Research with Children*. Maidenhead: Open University Press.

Steward, M., Barnfather, A., Magill-Evans, J., Ray, L. & Letourneau, N. (2011) An Online Support Intervention: perceptions of adolescents with physical disabilities. Brief report. *Journal of Adolescence*, 34(4), 795-800. http://dx.doi.org/10.1016/j.adolescence.2010.04.007

Swist, T., Collin, P., McCormack, J. and Third, A. (2015) Social Media and the Wellbeing of Children and Young People: a literature review. Perth, WA: Prepared for the Commissioner for Children and Young People, Western Australia.

Third, A., Bellerose, D., Dawkins, U., Keltie, E. & Pihl, K. (2014) *Children's Rights in the Digital Age: a download from children around the world.* Melbourne: Young and Well Cooperative Research Centre.

Titcomb, J. (2015) Teenagers Under 16 Will Need Parental Consent to Use Facebook and Email Under EU Laws, *Telegraph*, 14 December.

United Nations (1989) United Nations Convention on the Rights of the Child (UNCRC). Geneva: United Nations.

United Nations (2014) Committee on the Rights of the Child Report of the 2014 Day of General Discussion 'Digital Media and Children's Rights'.

Valkenburg, P.M. & Peter, J. (2007) Pre-adolescents' and Adolescents' Online Communication and Their Closeness to Friends, *Journal of Developmental Psychology*, 43(2), 267-277. http://dx.doi.org/10.1037/0012-1649.43.2.267

Valkenburg, P.M., Peter, J. & Schouten, A.P. (2006) Friend Networking Sites and Their Relationship to Adolescents' Wellbeing and Social Self-Esteem, *CyberPsychology and Behavior*, 9(5), 584-590. http://dx.doi.org/10.1089/cpb.2006.9.584

Varlas, L. (2011) Can Social Media and School Policies be 'Friends'?, *Policy Priorities*, 17(4). United Kingdom Government (1998) Human Rights Act.

Varnelis, K. (Ed.) (2008) *Networked Publics*. Boston, MA: MIT Press.

Wakefield, J. (2014). Do We Need to Rescue Our Kids from the Digital World? *BBC News*. http://www.bbc.com/news/technology-27501984 (accessed 21 July 2014).

Ward, V. (2013) Toddlers Becoming So Addicted to iPads They Require Therapy, *Telegraph*. http://www.telegraph.co.uk/technology/10008707/Toddlers-becoming-so-addicted-to-iPads-they-require-therapy.html (accessed 21 July 2014).

Whitbourn, M. (2014) The Tweet that Cost $105,000, *Sydney Morning Herald* http://www.smh.com.au/action/printArticle?id=5227509 (accessed 16 July 2014).

Woods, J. (2013) Should Parents Spy on Their Children's Emails and Texts? *Telegraph*, 22 January 2013. http://www.telegraph.co.uk/technology/internet/9815906/Should-parents-spy-on-their-childrens-emails-and-texts.html

Epilogue:
final reflections

This edited collection has presented some important considerations relating to examples of educational research practice informed by the CRC and the implementation and incorporation of children's rights in education across different international contexts, including Australia, Finland, Portugal, Sweden and the United Kingdom. Significantly, each contribution reaches beyond the specific geographical context in which it was written and speaks to global and wide-reaching implications for children's rights and educational research. From this rich vein of research and writing we would highlight six key messages for children's rights–informed educational research practice:

First, children's participation and active citizenship within and beyond the classroom is an important and worthwhile endeavour that can be enabled in a number of ways.

Second, children's rights should not be viewed as an 'add on' to educational research and practice, but instead, the principles should be embedded into the knowledge, skills, thinking and application of education.

Third, there is no 'single way' in which children's rights in educational practice can be incorporated. Instead, it should and can be viewed as a dynamic and continually evolving process that is contingent on the different contextual factors informing the place, space and time in which the education occurs.

Fourth, the collaborative, shared experiences between the teachers/researchers and children in each of the chapters demonstrate developing a shared understanding of rights in practice and what this might look like in different contexts.

Fifth, the concept of empowerment for both adults and children in seeking to enact children's rights in education and educational research is an important and worthwhile endeavour that requires greater attention. The importance of knowing and understanding how to enable children's rights in practice goes beyond merely knowing about children's rights in a theoretical sense. The authors in this collection provide a multitude of ways in which this can be facilitated. Despite different socio-economic statuses and contexts of relative wealth and poverty, children's rights and the implications for education remain both a priority and a possibility globally and locally.

Sixth, spaces can and should be created for the enactment of children's rights in education, but as a participant in Lúcio and Ferreira's study (this volume) puts it, 'children have the right to participation, but they also have the right to non-participation. They have the right to choose.'

Finally, we leave you with a challenge ... when considering children's rights, educational research and the UNCRC, what choices will you make?

Jenna Gillett-Swan & Vicki Coppock

Notes on Contributors

Vicki Coppock is Professor of Social Science: Childhood Studies and Mental Health at Edge Hill University, UK. During an academic career spanning 25 years Professor Coppock has built a national and international reputation for research and publications that focus on the investigation and social scientific analysis of theory, policy and professional practice in mental health. Her work problematises the dominance of the adult voice and the underrepresentation of the child voice in research, policy and practice and is characterised by a strong emphasis on asserting a positive children's human rights agenda. Her research practice is underpinned by a commitment to qualitative methodologies and participatory methods, including expertise in working with primary school-aged children as peer-researchers. Professor Coppock also has a research interest in gender and sexuality and has published in this field.

Jenna Gillett-Swan is a lecturer in education at the Queensland University of Technology, Australia. Her research is focused on children's rights, children's voice, and well-being. She also specialises in qualitative child-centred participatory research methodologies and finding ways for children to have a greater participatory role in contributing to matters that affect their lives. Jenna's interest in the role of digital technologies in the lives of networked children and young people stems from her participatory research practices where a range of communicative tools that children already choose to engage with outside of the research space can be utilised and their potential explored. Jenna is guest editor for the *Global Studies of Childhood* 2016 Special Issue, 'Children's Rights in the 21st Century Digital Age', and the *Asia Pacific Journal of Teacher Education* 2017 Special Issue, 'Exploring the Diversity of Pre-service and Beginning Teachers' Experiences through Multiple Lenses'.

Kristiina Kumpulainen is Professor of Education at the Department of Teacher Education, Faculty of Behavioural Sciences, University of Helsinki, Finland. She is also the founding member and the scientific director of the Playful Learning Center (www.plchelsinki.fi). She received her PhD in Education from the University of Exeter in 1994, focusing on children's collaborative writing with computers. She has held two distinguished scholarly positions awarded by the Academy of Finland. In the years 2006-09 she directed the national interdisciplinary research network on learning, CICERO Learning. She has also served as the Director of the Information and Evaluation Services Unit at the Finnish National Board of Education. Prof. Kumpulainen has been a visiting professor at the Institute of Education, University of Warwick, and at the University of California, Santa Barbara, USA. Prof. Kumpulainen's research focuses on tool-mediated learning and communication in various settings, including early childhood centres, schools, museums and teacher education settings. She has also addressed methodological questions in the analysis of social interaction in collaborative, creative and digital learning. Her current research centres on learning across contexts, play and playful learning, digital literacy, learner agency and identity, resilience, as well as visual participatory research.

Lasse Lipponen is a professor of education, with special reference to early childhood education, at the Department of Teacher Education, University of Helsinki, Finland. His research work is directed to compassion; children's agency; understanding children's experiences in their lifeworld with digital documentation and participatory research methods; and teacher education. Lipponen has authored over 100 research articles on teaching and learning. He is a co-founder of 'Playful Learning Center' (http://plchelsinki.fi), and a founding partner of Helsinki International Schools (heischools.com).

Joana Lúcio holds a PhD in Educational Sciences from the University of Porto, Portugal. She has coordinated and/or participated in several research-intervention projects in the field of local development, with a particular interest in non-formal and informal educational dynamics, as well as the role of associations, small and medium-sized enterprises and local government. She has taught mediation and conflict management in teacher training courses. She is a researcher at the Research Centre on Child Studies, University of Minho, Portugal. She has been collaborating with the European Educational Research Association since 2010, through its Network 14 – Communities, Families and Schooling in Educational Research (which she coordinated between 2012 and 2015). She has recently co-edited a special issue of the *European Educational Research Journal*, on the subject of 'Children as Members of a Community: citizenship, participation and educational development'.

Fernando Ilídio Ferreira holds a PhD in Child Studies from the University of Minho, Portugal, where he has been an Associate Professor since 2009. He teaches at the University's Institute of Education, at both the undergraduate and postgraduate levels, having also coordinated the practicum in pre-service basic school teacher training. He is a researcher at the Research Centre on Child Studies, University of Minho. For several years, he has been a consultant for a regional 'Teachers' Centre', as well as a local Priority Education cluster of schools. He has been a part of several national and international research projects, such as 'Teacher Induction: supporting the supporters of novice teachers in Europe', 'Leading Schools Successfully in Challenging Urban Contexts: strategies for improvement' and 'Teachers Exercising Leadership – Challenges and Opportunities'. He has authored more than a hundred books, book chapters and papers, addressing issues such as teacher education, school organisation, educational policies, community education, primary and pre-school education and childhood, in general. He has supervised several master's dissertations and doctoral theses in Education and Child Studies.

John I'Anson is Director of Initial Teacher Education in the Faculty of Social Sciences, University of Stirling, UK. He is Convenor for the Research in Children's Rights in Education Network at the European Conference on Educational Research (ECER). His research is focussed in the areas of children's rights, cultural difference, and aesthetic education.

Reetta Niemi is a lecturer at Viikki Teacher Training School, Faculty of Behavioural Sciences, University of Helsinki, Finland. She received her PhD from the University of Jyväskylä in 2009 focusing on participatory pedagogy in health education. After that her research has focused on developing participatory pedagogy through narrative learning projects. She has also addressed methodological questions in pedagogical action research. In her research, Reetta Niemi has developed visual participatory research methods in order to perceive children's meaningful learning experiences. Her research has also centred on understanding how children's meaningful experiences can help teachers to develop their practical theories and pedagogical actions in classrooms.

Louise G. Phillips is a lecturer in the School of Education at the University of Queensland, Australia where she teaches early years, arts and literacy education. Louise has been researching children's rights and citizenship for more than eight years. She is currently a recipient of a prestigious Spencer Foundation major grant for the project titled: 'Civic Action and Learning with Young Children: comparing approaches in New Zealand, Australia and the United States'. To enhance and innovate explorations of children's citizenship and civic engagement, Louise also collaborates with community cultural development artists and architects to explore opportunities for intergenerational participation in the public sphere.

Gordon Tait is an Associate Professor in the School of Cultural and Professional Learning at Queensland University of Technology. He has a background in Sociology and Physical Education and teaches in the areas of the sociology and philosophy of education, as well as education and the law. Gordon has published widely in the areas of cultural studies, sociology, philosophy and criminology. His current research interests surround applied philosophy and behaviour disorders as well as the sociology of death investigations.

Mallihai Tambyah is a Lecturer in Social Education in the Faculty of Education at Queensland University of Technology, Australia. In her doctorate she examined middle years teachers' conceptions of essential knowledge for social science education. Her research examines teacher professional identities, middle school teachers' approach to curriculum change, pre-service social science teachers' knowledge, teachers' work and initial teacher education. She is currently researching history teachers' use of digital/print fictional and information texts and how these texts shape their perspectives on national and civic identities in multicultural Australia.

Nina Thelander is a lecturer in educational work at Karlstad University, Sweden. Her main research interest concerns children's rights in education. Her doctoral thesis focused on school children's perspectives on children's rights in education in Kenya and Sweden. In addition to her interest in children's rights in education her research is also directed towards how children and childhood is constructed and regulated in various international educational contexts. Another research focus is in teaching and assessment issues especially from a child rights perspective. At the moment she is researching in a national project focusing on *what* children's human rights are in teaching and learning in Swedish schools. Moreover, she has participated and participates in various international partnerships and exchanges at the graduate level as well as at the undergraduate level.